CHINA
VIGNETTES

AN INSIDE LOOK AT CHINA

DOMINIC BARTON with MEI YE

This edition published in 2007
First Published in South East Asia
by Talisman Publishing Pte Ltd

ISBN 978-981-05-8091-9

Author's royalties will go to Non-Profit Partners Foundation (NPP)

Edited by Mary Fellowes and Glenn Leibowitz
Field interview support by Lu Hua
Original fiction edited and commissioned by Lu Jinbo, courtesy of Rongshu Publishing
Fiction translated by Sam Smith, courtesy of David Gettman, with writing support
by John Southard
Book design by Helm Keller
Original prepress by Gino Braun (Music in Motion, Munich, Germany) and
Christoph Findeiss.
Additional typesetting by Scientifik Graphics, Singapore.
Production management by Susanne Falk, supported by Jessice Xu.

Printed and bound by Markono Print Media Pte Ltd, Singapore

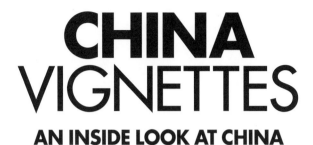

CHINA VIGNETTES

AN INSIDE LOOK AT CHINA

DOMINIC BARTON with MEI YE

Original contributions by

Yu Wen-Xin, Wang Xiao-Shan, YiYi, Old Cat, Xie Zheng-Yi, Jiang Fang-Zhou, Xiao Yi, Lin Chang-Zhi, An Chang-He, Liu Fang, You Fan, Enya, Liu Tong, Deng Weizhi, and Cao Peilin

Talisman

TABLE OF CONTENTS

I. Introduction

II. A Journey through China

III. Insiders' Reflections

IV. Appendixes

to the kind people who answered our questions and shared
their lives with us

I. INTRODUCTION

Why I did this
Foreword by Dominic Barton

This book is the product of a personal journey to gain a better and deeper understanding of the people of China and the transformation that is underway.

For the past three years, I have lived in Shanghai, in a townhouse near Xintiandi and an old Shikumen area. I work primarily with Chinese business executives and government officials, but I also spend a lot of time in other parts of Asia. I am an avid reader of Chinese history, and travel extensively in China during the major holidays.

About a year ago, after making a presentation to the members of the board of a U.S. company and their spouses on the "Myths and Realities of China," I was asked what all this transformation was like for the "average" Chinese family. I found myself responding with a battery of standard phrases: "... the incredible dynamism and energy of the people ...," "... government officials that seem more like GE executives than bureaucrats ...," "... the shocking gap between the rich and the poor ...," and so on. As I heard myself speaking, however, I began to wonder how much I really knew about living in China.

Much has been written about the remarkable economic transformation underway in China – massive infrastructure and private sector growth, reform of state-owned enterprises and the financial system, and the impressive leadership effectiveness of the Chinese Communist Party. Social issues are increasingly in the spotlight too: the colossal challenges of the rural-urban divide, social unrest, the lack of a social safety net. However, much of the analysis is written from an aggregated, synthesized, and often – I find – distant perspective.

I was keen on getting a more personal view of the changes underway, a better understanding of the historical context and the typical people in the midst of all this. So I began to scan the vast literature on China, seeing what I could learn. I quickly came across a number of worthwhile books from such authors as Jonathan Spence, Rana Mitter, and Ray Huang. The most interesting books for me have been historical. Two in particular stand out: "Chinese Characteristics" by Arthur H. Smith, a British missionary, who in the 1870s tried to systematically describe Chinese people in terms of 26 characteristics – a fairly bold and somewhat dangerous thing to do, although many of my Chinese colleagues say they are fairly accurate; and "1587 – A Year of no Significance" by Ray Huang, which offers an intimate view of life at the beginning of the decline of the Ming empire (the last time China was ascendant or dominant in the world) through the eyes of many leaders in the Court of the Emperor. (See Appendix for a list of my favorite books.)

But good as they were, I simply didn't feel pulled along by the "macro" approach that most authors employed. A chance encounter with "First Drafts: Eye Witness Accounts from our Past," by J.L. Granatstein and Norman Hillmer, suggested an alternative approach. This history of Canada uses personal letters and period newspaper articles to tell the story of major national milestones. This book led me to the idea of pursuing a deeper understanding of China's transformation by collecting personal views and stories from the people of China – about their daily lives, their culture, and the changes they are experiencing first-hand.

I began by exploring the Shikumen settlements not far from my home. Wandering through the narrow lanes of these low-slung buildings, designed in the 19th century to accommodate traditional Chinese living habits in a modernizing world, I encountered a very different side of Shanghai. Accompanied by an interpreter and often with one of my children, I chatted with clerks and customers in stores of every imaginable kind. We looked into tiny, one-room restaurants, baffled as to how they served two meals a day to hundreds of migrant workers from the construction sites nearby. Occasionally, we also got a glimpse of the sanitation system, generally no more than a garbage can on a rooftop.

Approach

Encouraged by these adventures, I became eager for much closer contact with a broader cross-section of "typical" Chinese people. I asked our research group and China Consumer Center at McKinsey to profile the typical occupations and geographic locations of people across China. They identified 43 occupations (see Appendix – pages 322-323) including, for example, rural doctors, taxi drivers, middle school teachers, farmers,  migrant workers, massage girls, factory workers, students, white collar private sector workers, and government officials. They lived in four major regions, from Shandong province and Beijing in the north, to Shanghai in the east, to Guangdong province in the south, to Sichuan province and Chongqing in the southwest. We also went to Lhasa in Tibet. I visited 30 people and their families, and selected 24 to profile in this book.

To identify people to meet and interview, I asked our China Consumer Center to nominate five individuals in each occupation category that we could contact. We then randomly selected 30 of them to profile. All but one accepted our request to interview them immediately.

We then asked each of the 30 to write a diary describing a typical day in their life – when they woke up, what they ate, who was with them, and all of the activities they undertook. Several were quite intimate in their descriptions. We also asked them to write about their desires, their worries, and what they were most proud of, and not so proud of. We then visited, interviewed, and observed them and their families. They also asked us a lot of questions. In some cases, we went back twice for more information. This often involved extensive travel. My son, Fraser, accompanied us on most trips as did my wife, Sheila, and my daughter, Jessica, on the more remote trips. The material we collected and recorded was rich and long – typically 25 pages per person – which was then turned into one of the vignettes you will find in this book.

The order of the vignettes follows the key geographic areas where we conducted interviews: Shandong province and the areas surrounding Beijing in the north; Shanghai and the surrounding areas in the east; Guangdong province in the south; and the areas surrounding Chongqing, and Sichuan province in the southwest.

Of course, these vignettes cannot capture the full richness and complexity of life in China today. I have not covered all the  geographies or occupation types, and there are surely significant differences among people in similar jobs or circumstances, and among those in the same towns or cities. As I look at the income levels of the individuals we have interviewed, there is a very wide range, but we are likely a little biased to the more affluent overall. But I hope these personal accounts of daily life offer a picture, feel, and understanding of the swirl of changes going on at this historic time. We use RMB for the income and budget, one RMB equals 13 cents or .10 Euro.

Interwoven with the profiles are short stories written by 13 of China's young, promising authors. They were asked to write a "day in the life of" fictional piece about one of the 43 jobs or occupation types we had identified at the outset of the process, and importantly, to interview several "real" people as background for their stories. Of the 30 writers we asked (identified by Lu Jinbo of the Rongshu Publishing Division of Bertelsmann China), 13 of their essays were included in the book. I hope these tales will give you another vantage point from which to view the changes going on in China today.

We also decided to interview a couple of well-known sociologists and political scientists to get their views on the patterns and issues they observe – sociology professor Deng Weizhi; and political science professor Cao Peilin.  They have conducted a large body of seminal research on the people and life in contemporary China, and have published many works on provocative and sometimes controversial social and political topics (for example, "the harmonious society," trust, political reform, ethics, HIV / AIDs, etc.). In the section Insiders' Reflections, we have included essays by each of them. I don't necessarily agree with all of their views, but I thought it would be useful for people to see what some of the advisors to the government and the Chinese Communist Party are thinking and how they express their perspectives.

In the Appendix, I have also included a number of charts with facts and figures on the social safety net, the rural-urban divide, and today's most popular magazines and television programs.

Themes

Though I hope you will take away your own themes and impressions of the people we have profiled here, let me briefly highlight some of the themes that resurfaced again and again for me:

Focus on children and education. The extent of the sacrifices undertaken by parents to make the lives of their children (in most cases, their only child) better. In most of the vignettes, parents focused their aspirations and worries on ensuring  that their child – or in a few cases children – had the foundation for a much better life than theirs. This involved moving the family to places with better schooling, working multiple jobs, and even sacrificing basic necessities like food to pay for educational expenses and extra-curricular tutoring and training.

The workload and pressure on children "to perform" was also astounding. Most of the children we met, including those as young as six years old, spent five hours a day beyond their school day either studying or being tutored. All were stressed by the heavy workload and high expectations placed on them.

The work ethic – drive, perseverance, and ambition. The commitment, energy, and doggedness to improving the life and potential for the family unit was astounding. The long work hours – at least six days a week, 12 hours a day – for most of the people we interviewed; the conditions in which some people live (one migrant worker shares a bed with a co-worker in the same room that houses seven other workers); the lack of adequate lighting; the cold; the complete lack of sanitation in many of the dwellings – all were quite staggering.

Lack of social safety net. For most of the people we interviewed, their biggest fear or concern (beyond their child getting into a good school) was not having enough money for a medical emergency. All families, except those of the government workers who had some health coverage, saved a large proportion of their salary (for example, 25 percent) to cover potential health problems for a direct family member or relative. Without money, you get no treatment. Most also worried about having sufficient funds for when they became too old to work, relying mainly on the hope that their child or children would be able to take care of them in time of need.

Strength of the family unit. Loyalty, responsibility, and care for parents were critical. Most husbands and wives acted as partner-teams. I am sure, that these were not always marriages of bliss and happiness, but the care and commitment of spouses, and the equal roles played in housework and caring for the family, were quite surprising to me.

Views on authority. There was little conversation on the role of government or the Communist Party – not  so much because people were uncomfortable talking about it; in fact, people were very open about their likes, concerns, and complaints. They seemed to treat the "authorities" like the weather – beyond their control, roughly predictable, capable of wreaking havoc from time to time – and there was little anyone could do about it. Most people focused on the issue of whether the government could provide jobs – job security was a source of constant worry. There was a sense that the Party was there to provide stability and opportunity by promoting general economic growth.

The Cultural Revolution. The impact of the Cultural Revolution cannot be underestimated. The impact it seems to have had on "trust" and "community" in the families we interviewed was considerable. All families I met believed that the only people they could trust were themselves and their individual family members. One man was quite obsessed with the question of whether man is "inherently evil" – a view he had come to believe from his experiences during the Cultural Revolution. This period of time (1966-1976) is not taught or talked about at school or much in families, but the impact and consequences still linger on, and I believe that there will continue to be substantial second-order effects on Chinese society for some time.

Corruption. Many of the people we interviewed complained about corruption – especially in the health care system, but also among local government officials. There was a sense that the situation might be improving because there is much more Party focus and media  transparency on this issue – but there is still a long way to go.

Views on foreigners. There was a benign or rather indifferent view toward foreigners among those we interviewed. It may just have been that there were much higher priorities – such as jobs, children, education – but whenever I asked about their views on the U.S., Europe, Taiwan, and Japan, they did not display much energy or passion, apart from some comments on the Japanese, with which there appears to be some significant underlying tension; on Taiwan, i.e., "it is part of the Motherland;" and to some extent, on the U.S. ("a bully," but "appears to be a great place to live"). Many seemed to have heard and think highly of the education and health care systems in the U.S. or Australia, especially when compared to that in China. Since the vast majority of the people we interviewed have never been outside of China, and have very limited interactions with foreigners in China, they form their opinions and views mainly through the influence of official channels (TV, newspapers, etc.).

I wish you a good journey.

Acknowledgements

I would like to thank Mei Ye, who was a true partner in this process from beginning to end. She has a terrific ability to get to know people quickly and to build trust. She has also been a wonderful collaborator in this whole process. Thank you also for the passion you brought to this work!

I would also like to thank Holm Keller, who was head of Bertelsmann China, and who is a longstanding friend, for his insightful and tireless collaboration on this book, especially during the formative stages and the closing stages. He encouraged me to professionalize my approach, for which I am very grateful, and provided a wealth of ideas and leads in many areas, especially in finding our young authors. Lu Jinbo of the Rongshu Publishing Division of Bertelsmann China also provided substantial help in identifying and guiding the young authors of the tales.

To my wife, Sheila, son, Fraser, and daughter, Jessica, thank you for your support in this hobby, and for your companionship during the countless excursions and longer trips we took together in creating this book. Your enthusiasm and curiosity added a vital dimension to our discussions with the various families.

Critical here for all of us were, of course, our interpreters who with great skill and endless patience allowed the many interchanges to take place smoothly and painlessly. Also, a huge thank you to Katharine Bowerman, my assistant, who scheduled all of our trips, typed countless drafts of the profiles, and also provided helpful input.

I would also like to thank Mary Fellowes, who patiently read through very broken translations of our interviews, provided helpful critical comments while maintaining "the voice" of the people interviewed, and who prevented this from becoming a one thousand page book.

This is a personal initiative, not a McKinsey book, but I am grateful to Shamus Mok and the people in McKinsey's China Consumer Center who provided invaluable help in narrowing down the occupation types for our interviews, and who helped as well identify specific individuals for interviews, and to Glenn Leibowitz, a good friend who provided terrific input on synthesizing the vignettes.

Finally, I want to thank the 30 kind people who took the time to record their thoughts about their day, to respond cheerfully to the many, many questions we had, and who treated us with the most endearing hospitality. You are the heart of this book.

Age 54 · **Occupation** Farmer in Shandong · **Family** Husband, two grown sons · **Home** Three-bedroom, one-story house on a 240 m² lot · **Free time** Watching TV, visiting neighbors, doing handicrafts · **Monthly income (RMB)**

BIAN XIUKUI

Farmer
Shandong

Personal – 200; Household – 1,400+ (includes 1,200 from sons) · **Household budget (RMB)** Housing/Utilities – 100; Education – 0; Parent support – 0; Health care – 1,000; Food/Clothing/Other – 300; Savings – 0

BIAN XIUKUI'S DIARY

7:00 – In the winter, when we don't have much field work, we get up around 7 a.m. Otherwise, it's around 4. As soon as we get up, I make breakfast, and my husband goes out to feed the chickens. We like having homemade noodles for breakfast, along with vegetables.

8:00 – After breakfast, I often do some sewing, like making clothes for myself. Sometimes I make shoes, and other times, decorated pillows for children. Then I usually go out and chat with my neighbors. I have lots of good friends here. Some are older, some younger. We get along really well and have great fun together.

12:00 – I make and serve lunch. We like buns and having several different vegetable dishes, sometimes with dumplings. The dumplings can be filled with almost anything – vegetables or Chinese radish with pork, for example. They're always delicious.

13:00 – I do the dishes most of the time, while my husband is outside working, doing welding at a construction site or something like that. Now he only takes jobs nearby, although he used to work in far-away places, like Jinan. My health is not very good, so I often take a nap after lunch and sleep for two hours or so.

15:00 – Afterwards, I go outside or maybe watch TV. We really enjoy going out and visiting our neighbors. We have so may things to talk about, like our children, the old people, and family affairs.

18:00 – For dinner we have rice congee, buns, and several other dishes. After dinner, we often watch TV for a while. (We don't have any movie theaters around here.) Or we may go out or have friends and neighbors over for a chat. In the summer, I like to play cards with friends and stay up until 9 or 10 p.m. But in the winter, it's very cold, so I go to sleep early, by 8 p.m. at the latest.

A CHAT WITH BIAN XIUKUI

Your house is very nice. When did you build it?

In 2003. My sons earn a lot and helped us pay for it. They both work in Beijing. Our village is growing nicely. About a third of the people here have built houses over the past few years. It's much the same with them. Their grown children work in the city and send money home so their parents can build homes.

Everyone seems to live close together here in the north. Was it always like this?

When I was a child, everybody – simple farmers, landowners, and rich farmers – lived close together. There were good houses, bad houses, large lots, small lots – all of them were close together.

Did you attend school?

Yes, but not for very long. We lived in a poor rural area, and not many people went to school back then. I did finish the third grade, which was more than most. In those days, there were too many kids and not enough food. Parents didn't have the money for school, and also they needed them to work on the farm. Less than a third of the children my age went to junior or senior high school. Life was hard.

It seems that you have many TV channels here.

We have cable TV. I don't know how to read, so when I'm home, the TV is on all the time. The Beijing TV station has news and interesting legal cases.

When did you family acquire land to farm on its own?

I think in the 1980s. There wasn't much land available. You could get roughly 1 mu (about 660 m²) for each worker in the family, so we received 4 mu. We planted wheat in the winter and corn in the summer. Things would be very busy in June, but there wasn't much to do inbetween – just watering, fertilizing, and spraying.

How did you sell your wheat and corn?

Through middlemen. We also used to have to pay taxes on the land. They were very high. I think about 200 yuan per mu every year.

How does your family handle the farm work today?

Planting doesn't take much time, and we work with machines now.

Do you usually have a good harvest?

We have quite good harvests here. Now, since my sons left, we only have 2 mu, which brings in about 2,000 yuan a year. That's our main income.

Is that enough for you?

Far from it. We depend very much on our sons now. They helped pay for our house and also help cover our regular expenses. We grow most of our food, but there are other costs, especially medical. We don't have insurance, and my health is not very good. I spent about 10,000 yuan of my son's income last year for my medical treatment. I've heard that medical insurance is becoming available in rural areas, but I don't understand much about it. I might not be able to get coverage anyway.

What is the illness?

Arthritis. At first, I tried to treat it myself. Then, for almost two years, I went to the county hospital. Last year, I went to a big hospital in Beijing and after one year, I feel much better. The doctors there are more skilled.

Do you have any other worries?

No, I feel really good now. My sons are very kind to me and that makes me very happy. I'm just waiting for grandchildren!

How often do you visit your sons?

Once in a while. Sometimes I stay with them for two months, sometimes six weeks. I come back when I start to miss home and my friends in the village.

What do you think of Beijing?

Beijing is fine. But I don't like going up and down the stairs, and there are also too many cars. I don't know many people there, so I just stay at home and watch TV or do my handicrafts.

Do you follow current events?

No, mostly because I don't really understand them.

What about the big problems in rural areas that are so much in the news?

I did see something about that on TV. All I know is that some policies are better now. We farmers don't have to pay taxes now. That's a good policy, and I'm happy about that. But I don't know much about the way the country is developing. I just sense that China is better off and more stable now.

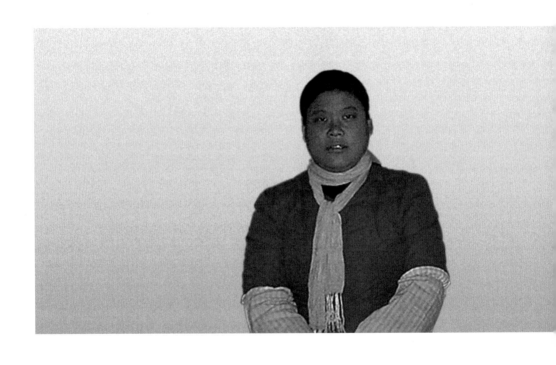

Age 31 · **Occupation** Country doctor in Shandong · **Family** Husband, seven-year-old son · **Home** Three-bedroom, one-story house on a 240 m² lot · **Free time** Watching TV, helping with homework · **Monthly income (RMB)** Personal

Han Lanzheng

Country doctor
Shandong

1,500; Household – 8,000 · **Household budget (RMB)** Housing/Utilities – 300; Education – 200; Parent support – n/a; Health care – 0; Food/ Clothing/Other – 1,500; Savings – 6,000

星期一

　　清早睁开眼睛就开始忙了碌了的一天。做饭
是孩子上学后，开始忙于门诊上的几个病人。干我们这一行
卫生事业，特别是在农村，又是一个私人门诊，对于病人必
须小心、细心、安全用药，才能为病人解除痛苦。

　　我一个普普通通的农村妇女，一天忙于缠手的几
个病人，还有许多多在门诊不能诊断的病，必须
到上级医院借助辅助检查，才能确诊的病历。
我上午输只几个输液的病人，还有几个去上级医院
确诊的病，我就得一个一个的去和她们到上级医院
去检查。

　　我作为一个医疗工作者，连接孩子，做饭、洗衣做
家务都顾不上，匆忙中吃过饭以后，一个恶冒引起发烧病人
输完液后，我去药材公司去提一些缺少的药物，
晚上有许多，忙于病人晚上10点以后休息。

第　页

7:00 – After getting up, I cooked breakfast for my family and sent my son to school. Then I walked to my clinic.

8:00 – I began seeing patients from the moment I opened the door of the clinic. I see about eight to ten patients a day. Country doctors can only help alleviate people's aches and pains. I see plenty of patients I can't diagnose or treat, and there were several cases like that today. I accompanied them to the hospital for more tests, as I normally do.

10:00 – After I finished with these patients, I went on to another hospital, where I had a patient who was turning out to be very difficult to treat. We had been to the hospital together several times, but she was still not well.

12:00 – Back at the clinic, I ate lunch while waiting for a patient to finish his IV and then went to the druggist quickly to get some medicine I had run out of. In the afternoon, I saw a patient who had a cold and put him on an IV. Then I saw a 90-year-old patient who had been having more and more trouble with digestion. I suspected some gastric bleeding and put him on an IV.

16:00 – After seeing several more patients, I went to pick up my son and made dinner. As a country doctor, I don't always have time to pick up my child, cook meals, wash clothes, or do housework. But today I had more time.

18:00 – After dinner, I saw a few other patients. It's like this every day, every month of the year.

22:00 – I went to bed and hoped I would not get awakened by a patient in the night. I'm on duty 24 hours a day or so it seems.

A CHAT WITH HAN LANZHENG

Dr. Han, how did you become a doctor with your own clinic?
You don't have to call me "Doctor." People just call me "Mother of Tong Hao." I went to Binzhou Medical School after junior middle school and

spent three years there – the first one for theory, the next two for practical training. I took the county exam after graduation in 1994 and received my certificate to open a clinic. Many people from the country, like me, have done the same thing. I worked with my grandfather at first, and then began to run the clinic on my own. Most of my work is in internal medicine, pediatrics, and gynecology. I don't do any suturing here.

Do you own this building?
No, I rent it. The Health Bureau requires a clinic to have at least 40 m², so another doctor and I share this space, each with 20 m². But I'm going to move the clinic to my home next year because the dispensary here is not up to standard. I don't have anything built yet, but I am going to start working on it soon.

How do you usually diagnose people?
I analyze a patient's symptoms and prescribe medicine accordingly. In rural areas like this, people usually come to a local clinic first unless they have something very serious, in which case they go straight to the hospital. I once saw an old woman who came in at 6 a.m., an 88-year-old grandmother. I suspected a heart attack and told her to go to the hospital. My diagnosis was confirmed there, but she died the next day. I learned from that experience that some conditions have to be treated immediately.

How do you charge your patients?
People who receive IVs pay a one-time minimum fee of 3 yuan. IVs for patients with fever cost about 20, and medications cost 5 or 6 yuan.

I usually see only eight to ten patients a day. The old woman you just saw bought a special bandage for chapped hands costing 1.5 yuan, and the other woman was here for an injection to treat a gynecological problem.

Is your clinic open every day?
Yes. I usually start work around 8 a.m., but I'm on call 24 hours a day. Sometimes people even come to my house. I don't have much time for housework, and free time comes in bits and pieces. Although I really work hard, I am still too fat!

How do you get paid?

We earn our living by selling medicine and treating patients. My annual income is usually at least 10,000, and sometimes as much as 20,000 to 30,000. Doctors who give scalp injections to children or suture patients with injuries make much more. Even though I'm not making a lot, my family is doing all right because my husband runs a taxi and transportation service with his van and can make 70,000 or 80,000 a year.

Do you plan to keep working as a country doctor?
You have to take risks in this profession, but of course I'll continue. We get training from the Health Bureau once every six months, sometimes more often. And then there are occasional exams, which are very hard. But at least they don't take that long – only half a day.

What are your expectations for your son?
I hope he will get a college degree and a high-paying job in the city. After junior high school here, he will go to the county senior high school. High school is more accessible to the general population than in my time. Only about 5 percent of the students at my school went on to high school. Conditions are much better today.

Is there anything that particularly worries you in your life?

I worry that I fight too much with my husband. I'm not very even-tempered, and he is. That's a small worry, though. I want my son to be very successful. We grew up during the good years of this country and under the Communist Party we don't have any really big concerns. I just hope no one gets sick in my family and that we are spared misfortunes. A safe and stable life is enough for me.

Do you observe any tensions in the doctor-patient relationship?

Well, when patients don't see the effects of the medicine I prescribe, they may talk about it behind my back or confront me. But the relationship is basically okay. People will come again if they think you're good. Otherwise, they can go elsewhere, though they may have to wait a long time for a city doctor. There have also been malpractice cases there. That's why I am so cautious. I treat people only when I know what I'm doing.

Are you interested in current events?

I don't have much time for that. We do subscribe to some newspapers. That's required, though we never seem to have time to read them. I am a candidate for Communist Party membership now. The Party Secretary came to me personally and asked me to submit an application.

Are you concerned about the rural issues identified by the government?

We are ordinary people and not really concerned about those things. We're doing fine here, mainly because my husband is doing well with his transportation business. In many other

rural areas, transportation is not so well developed, and people are still very poor.

What do you think about the world outside China?
I see on TV what's going on outside the country, like the war in Iraq. But it's not much use being concerned about that sort of thing.

What kind of books do you like to read?
I rarely read books. I read medical literature and Health Bureau booklets when I can. And I have to read to prepare for exams.

Do you have a lot of interaction with the County Health Bureau?
You have to go there for training every year, and you also have to pay them quite a bit to take exams. I pay about 2,000 a year for various things – like this sign, which cost 100 yuan. They said I had to buy it and hang it up.

What do you think about the health conditions and medical care in the rural areas?
Things are getting better but both are still in a poor state in general. Farmers can usually afford treatment for minor illnesses, but if they become very sick, they can be in serious trouble.

THE GRANDPARENTS' TALE
by Yu Wen-Xin

The sound of coughing from outside wakes me up. It is 5:30 a.m. My eyes only half-open, I see that the wooden door is already unbolted, and against the hazy light of dawn I can just make out Grandpa collecting firewood in the yard. Yesterday, I left the city to come and spend my day off with my grandparents. They have tilled the land here in the northwest of China their whole lives.

Here, things are very different. Where I slept last night, for instance, is an earthen platform bed. Such beds are a peculiarity of this region. On a cold winter night, a fire can be lit under the platform for warmth. I slept fine without one last night, though it is already frosty and cold, as it usually is here in October.

Grandpa has on a long overcoat of thick, rough cotton. He has come inside to light the stove. On top of the stove is a small kettle, which he fills with well water and tea leaves. When the kettle starts to hiss, Grandpa unhurriedly pours the boiling tea into a cup and then adds more water to the kettle. He takes his time drinking the cup of steaming tea, holding the cup close to his chest between sips.

Grandpa has bronchitis, and a few cups of hot tea in the morning seem to make his breathing easier. He refuses to take medicine, let alone go to the hospital. But, despite his condition, he won't stop smoking. His first cup of tea finished, Grandpa lights his pipe. Between puffs, he softly sings a song I recognize – a folk song from the region.

Through the open door I can see that dawn has broken into a pale gray day. Still singing, Grandpa puts his wicker basket onto his back. Throwing my clothes on, I walk with him through the alleys of the village, along the meandering paths into the hills, to a large cornfield. By this time, the sunlight is starting to prevail over the gray. A few other villagers are already here, also picking corn.

Following behind, I watch how Grandpa grasps the thick stem with one hand, while his other seeks the right hold on the ear. Then, with a crisp snap, he breaks it off and throws it over his shoulder into the wicker basket on his back. Soon he has fallen into a rhythm, and the ears are flying one after another into the basket. I find it hard to believe that he can still do this at his age. Soon, my two uncles arrive to help. They also have shares in the field. When all have filled their baskets — what in my eyes has been a good morning's work — we start for home. I sneak a glance at my watch — only 8:30 a.m.

When we get home my aunt is drawing water from the well. Seeing Grandpa with the heavy basket, she puts down her bucket and eases it off his back. (I should have thought of that.) Grandma is feeding the pigs, which grunt loudly as they eat. Grandpa tells her to add more boiled soy beans to the feed. "We need them to grow fatter," he tells me. "We're counting on them for New Year's." He means to keep half the meat for the family and to sell the rest. Grandpa goes to wash up with water from the well. When he has finished, we all sit down to breakfast.

We eat a thick soup of wheat flour, dumplings, fried shredded potatoes, and pickled vegetables. The smaller grandchildren come running to play the game of feeding Grandpa. Taking one bite from here and another bite from there, Grandpa clearly enjoys their attention. My uncles spread thick coats of homemade noodles with fried chili onto the dumplings.

After breakfast the grandchildren go off to school. Grandpa says, children in the mountain villages finally have schools to go to, but their parents still have worries. They worry if they aren't successful in school, but they also worry if they are successful, because then they won't want to come back and work the land. Most parents would rather borrow money, though, than put an early end to their children's school career.

Breakfast over, Grandpa and my uncles hurry back to the cornfield. They have to harvest all the corn in these two days to make room for the wheat. A few days ago, they harvested the apples, but they didn't get a good price because too many families have also planted apple trees in the region. In a few days, they will be digging up the potatoes and cutting the sorghum. Grandpa and my uncles hope to get a better price for those crops. My grandparents' house is in drastic need of repairs.

"After all our ups and downs, your Grandpa is still an optimistic and a determined man," my Grandma tells me. I am now on my way with Grandma to the village temple, which the villagers call the Temple of Three Sages. In these parts they have always worshipped saints, the origins of whom have disappeared into the mists of antiquity. In this village, then, it is not a Bodhisattva or a Buddha who are revered, but three sages who were known to perform miracles.

In the temple, Grandma lights three incense sticks and starts to softly mumble her prayers. A young Buddhist monk with half-closed eyes is rhythmically tapping a "muyu" (a wooden fish), while Grandma kneels down on the rush cushions and bows, touching her forehead to the ground three times. I am moved by the spirit of the temple and begin praying for the well-being of my family.

On our way back to the house I ask Grandma if she is still in love with Grandpa. Grandma says that she doesn't know exactly what "love" means. "Anyway," she says, "I've stuck by him all my life." I ask her what she prayed for. Grandma says that she prayed to the Three Sages for this coming year to be free of drought and for a good harvest, a son for my aunt, and safety for all family members working away from home. She says that she prayed that all would soon come home for a reunion.

When we get home, my small aunt has already returned from taking lunch to Grandpa and my uncles in the field. Pleased with herself, she says she brought them extra vegetables and meat today because she knew they would be very hungry after so much work.

In the afternoon, my other aunt braids soaked wheat stalks and makes straw hats from them. This brings in some extra money. This aunt is good with her hands. She can also make miniature baskets and animals with these braids. Modestly, she tells me that once some foreigners from the city had seen her handiwork at the fair and praised it highly. My aunt says that if she had the money, she would set up a small workshop and make all kinds of things from straw.

As she works, she speaks of how my grandparents are getting very old and that she and my uncle want to make more money so that they won't have to go on working so hard. "Neither of your grandparents is well, but they won't go to the hospital. Your Grandpa works in the field every season. Even when the plowing and harvesting is done and there's nothing to worry about, he still goes to take a look. He says he cannot live without his field."

At 7 p.m., I stand beside my aunt, helping her cook dinner. She uses a handmade bellows to get the wood burning nicely in the earthen stove. While my aunt rolls the dough and slices it into thin strands, I ladle juice from the pickled vegetables – a local specialty – into the big iron cauldron.

We are just finishing our work on the hot noodle soup when one of my uncles arrives in his truck with Grandpa and a full load of corn. Everyone, children and all, starts unloading the truck, laying the ears out in the yard, on the outside stairs, and on the window sills. Some ears even get hung under the eaves in the front of the house. My aunt takes some of the smaller ones and puts them in a pot to cook.

The table is set up over the bed where I sleep. Grandpa sits with his legs crossed, eating noodles and fried eggs with chili, and drinking home-made spirits with my uncles. All of us drink to Grandpa's health, and we praise him – that today he did the work of a man in his prime. Our aunt tells everyone that the money from her older brother has come. He hopes you take care of your health, my aunt says to her parents. Grandpa whispers to me that he is not afraid of old age or death.

Someone turns on the TV to watch "The Same Song," which is a favorite of the children. Another musical program follows, but then Grandpa yells out for it to be changed – he does not approve of the provocative dancing. So we watch the weather forecast on the local channel: tomorrow will be another sunny, cool day. "Excellent!" cries Grandpa and drinks another glass of spirits. "A perfect day for drying corn!"

Yu Wenxin, who studied in the Party School of the CPC and Nankai University, works in the media business.

Age 37 · **Occupation** Taxi driver in Beijing · **Family** Wife, seven-year-old son · **Home** 90 m², three-bedroom condominium · **Free time** Visiting with parents and in-laws, watching children's TV programs with son, exercising, reading the newspaper, cooking, helping with homework · **Monthly income (RMB)**

Xu Zhiguo

Taxi driver
Beijing

Personal – 3,500; Household – 3,500 · **Household budget (RMB)** Housing/
Utilities – 2,000; Education – 300; Parent support – 0; Health care – 200;
Food/Clothing/Other – 800; Savings – 200

　　"太阳当空照，花儿对我笑，小鸟说，早早早，你为什么背上小书包，我去上学校，天天不迟到，爱学习，爱劳动，长大要为祖国立功劳。"

　　这是一首我们儿时都会唱的歌，它陪伴了我快乐的童年，30年过去了我依然很喜欢唱这支歌，也喜欢唱给我的小孩听，现在我的小孩也会唱这支歌。

　　我叫许志国，38岁，是北京北汽九龙一名出租司机，我从事出租这一行已8年，说起出租司机工作，我感受很多，先说几行之前，在原单位下岗后，觉得自己有几年驾驶经验，就学了出租汽车驾驶证，来到北汽出租汽车公司开上了出租车，一干上才知道，这一行真的很辛苦，有很多人都认为出租车的工作很随便，每天开着车游览着都市风景，和乘客聊着天，就把钱挣了，包括

北京市电车公司印刷厂出品　九四・六

我以前也这么想过，可一接触，才觉得想法和实际差距很大。出租司机的工作是："时间 十 会理数 十 治安防范 十 交通安全 十 规范化服务"等于4久几。

1. 先说工作时间。大多数的出租司机会早6点到晚8点，工作时大约在12—15小时之间。我个人因初干出租车3年中，经验不足，每天工作时间长，收入并不多，干得愉疲劳。现身体也有些小问题。在后几年的工作中，自己意识到健康是第一位的，所以每天的工作时间会少做2个小时，这样每天早上6.30分起床，夏天会早一点，在小区公园里锻炼30分钟。我们工作是坐在车上，活动机会很少，加强体育锻炼对于我们来说非常必要，在锻炼中，主要是活动腿、腰和颈椎。我先做快步走，接下来做弯腰动作，然后做

XU ZHIGUO'S DIARY

6:30 – I start my day singing a song from my childhood, as I usually do, which goes something like this: "The sun is shining above/The flowers are smiling at me/I love study and labor/I will do good things for my country/When I am all grown up." I get dressed in my sports clothes and go to the park for my morning exercise. I usually exercise for half an hour, starting with speed walking and then stretching, especially my legs and neck.

7:15 – At home, I take a shower and have breakfast. After breakfast, my wife takes our son to school. If the weather is bad, I take him because my wife only has a bike. Whenever I take him, I set aside five minutes to talk with him in the car before he gets out. We have been teaching him to be responsible from the time he was three. We never spank him, but we don't spoil him either. We follow certain principles and hope he will benefit from them all his life.

8:00 – I drive a regular client to work Monday through Friday. She works for a multinational company. I take her to her office building, keeping an eye out for people waiting for a taxi. There are a lot of office buildings there, and taxis are always in short supply. We have all kinds of ways of finding passengers in Beijing – queuing near airports, restaurants, office buildings, parks, residential neighborhoods, and train stations. Or we may just "sweep the road," which is taxi driver talk for cruising for passengers without a fare.

12:00 – I ate lunch out, as usual, since it's too far to drive home. I sometimes eat in a cafeteria in one of the office buildings. They tend to be reasonably priced and good. After lunch, I rest for half an hour in the car and drink a little water.

13:00 – I picked up my 12th fare of the day. Some people think being a taxi driver is easy. You earn money just driving around, enjoying the scenery and chatting with people. I even used to believe that myself.

But no longer. It's really hard work. Most of us drive 250 to 300 miles on an average day, which can mean 12 to 15 hours in the car. I drive more like 10 to 12 hours a day because my health is more important to me. Being a taxi driver can be dangerous too. Sometimes people call for a taxi late in the evening, then have the driver take them to some desolate place where they rob and murder them. It's an old trick, but there have been several cases like that just recently. One driver was only 24, a newlywed of two months and in his first week on the job. Very sad.

21:00 – I came home and showered, while my wife warmed up some dinner for me. She and our son had already eaten dinner, since they never know exactly when I'll be home. After dinner, I cleaned up my car. I think it's important to show respect for your customers, and keeping the car clean is one way of doing that. My work finished, I sat down with my wife and watched some TV. I felt happy at the end of my day.

A CHAT WITH XU ZHIGUO

How long have you been in this business?

I've been driving a taxi for more than eight years. I didn't go to high school, so I started working right after middle school, like a lot of people my age. I started working in cattle breeding in the suburbs south of Beijing, but 13 years later I got laid off as a result of the social

reform. I was married and had to support my family, so a friend in the taxi business helped me get a job.

How is business?

When I started, I could gross 3,000 yuan a month without any difficulty. But this is more difficult now. Now the traffic is very heavy, but my experience helps. I don't waste as much time cruising around or

waiting at places with only a few customers. So my net earnings have increased over time.

You have a son in school now?

Yes, he's in the first grade. After he was born, my wife went back to work for a while, but after we moved here, she had to stop so she could take him back and forth to kindergarten. When he starts the third grade, she's planning to go back to work. She's bored just staying at home.

Do you own this apartment?

Yes, I bought it two years ago with a private loan from relatives. The apartment is new, but it isn't luxurious. We bought it so our son could go to school in this district. In fact, we moved to the city in the first place for the sake of his education.

How is he doing overall?

He's doing well. We have certain rules at home, and he is good about obeying them. He goes to bed at a certain time and is not allowed to watch TV from Monday to Thursday. He does his homework right away, and after that, he practices and plays the electronic keyboard. He enjoys that and is taking lessons for it at school. We have put our hearts into bringing him up. After all, 80 percent of child-rearing is already over by the time a child is seven.

Where did you learn about bringing up children?
Over the years, I have had many people in my taxi, including experts in preschool education. I'm a fast learner when it comes to other people's experience. I don't mean to boast, but I try to use what I've learned. A lot of kids my son's age can't even dress themselves. That's a problem we don't have. When he goes into the fourth grade, I plan to train him in study habits.

You are very attentive to your child.
Most of the time, I can even read his thoughts from his face or his voice. While he was washing the other day, he called "Papa," and it sounded different to me than usual. So I asked him what the matter was, and it turned out he had a sore throat.

Do you talk about politics with your passengers?
A lot of taxi drivers complain about the government, but I don't. There's no point in it. You just get upset. However, a couple of years ago, on the anniversary of the founding of the Communist Party, taxi drivers went on strike in Beijing because fuel prices had risen three times that year. In the end, the government gave us an allowance of 320 yuan per month to help cover these rising costs.

Was it an organized strike?
No. Beijing is very big. It wouldn't be easy to organize so many taxi drivers. When we heard that there would be a strike on the first of July,

everybody got involved, just the way people did for the anti-Japan demonstration. Word spread fast without any organization at all.

What other issues do you care about?
We taxi drivers are very concerned about political issues and policies that affect us, especially in Beijing. We listen to the radio and keep current on national affairs, such as who is visiting a foreign country, who has come to China, and what such visits mean to China.

Do you have medical insurance?
Yes. I pay outpatient expenses up to 2,000 yuan and get reimbursed for 50 percent of anything over that. For hospital stays, I only have to pay 10 percent. My son has insurance through the school, but my wife has none. After I pay off the mortgage, we want to start saving for retirement.

What other plans do you have for the future?
I like this job very much. It somehow suits my personality. But I can only do it for another five years at most. I'd like to open a small business after that, to get a shop and do catering. I enjoy cooking a lot.

What worries do you have about the future, if any?
Compared to the hardships of my parents' generation, we really don't have many worries. During the ten years of the Cultural Revolution, not only my family but all of society was totally stopped. Now my parents are reasonably healthy, and my wife has several brothers who help take care of her parents. My brother is also doing very well. I have been very filial to my parents. I show my care towards my parents by calling them on the phone, visiting them at weekends, and chatting with them.

What expectations do you have for your son?
My wife and I talk about this a lot. We want our son to do well on the college entrance exam. If he passes, there shouldn't be any problem.

I've been saving money for the past five years and should have enough to pay for his college tuition. I want my son to learn as much as he can, but I also want him to know how to act as a human being in society. If you are in touch with society, you can live and work in it successfully.

What do you think about foreigners?

I have very good feelings about foreigners. I have met a lot of them over the years, and some have even been able to speak fluent Chinese. Foreign people are much more direct than we are. If I have an appointment with you tonight and don't want to go, I will find all kinds of excuses rather than just telling you the truth. I think foreign people are just more honest with each other.

What about foreign countries themselves?

Well, the U.S. is a country with a strong sense of human rights. And the

economies of many foreign countries are generally much stronger than ours. Perhaps it's because they have fewer people. In Norway the cost of education – from kindergarten to university – is covered by the government. Our country can't match that. But we're no longer as far behind as we were 15 or 20 years ago. Of course, there's still much corruption in China, but going out and demonstrating against it won't help. Hu Jintao and Wen Jiabao are at least continuing to pursue corrupt officials.

Do you have confidence that the government will succeed here?

Though we have corruption in our country, I believe we should be optimistic. I've never complained about the government to my passengers and I won't, because there's no use in complaining – that would only make you worry more. Taxis provide visitors with a "window" on Beijing. To foreign guests, we represent China with our taxi services.

THE GARBAGE PICKER'S TALE
by Wang Xiao-Shan

Our alarm clock is the 4:20 a.m. train: It feels like it's roaring straight through the house. This is no exaggeration. Although to call this a house is an exaggeration. It is one of many shanties along the railway tracks.

It is 4:20 a.m., and I tell myself, as I do every day, that we ought to get up even earlier. But Damao and Ermao already cry out for more sleep when we wake them. It is still dark as my wife and I stumble around getting dressed. We have to be out before the garbage trucks arrive.

My wife lost her job as a cleaning lady in an office because she broke someone's cup. She was wiping a desk and accidentally knocked it to the floor. Now we both pick garbage. We worry every day about our children, who trail along with us in our work. I hurry them along now. We have to be out before the garbage trucks arrive.

There's no fence between our house and the railway tracks. But the children have nowhere else to play. We call the railroad "the manslaughter machine." Every month at least one person is killed around here. Only a few days ago I had to pull Ermao, who is five, out of the path of a train.

I despaired. "Crushed by a train, or crushed by life," I asked my wife, "What's the difference?" Hundreds of us garbage pickers live alongside this section of the railroad. We call it Garbage Town, though not for much longer. The land here has been rezoned as an industrial park. We will all be resettled, again.

We have been resettled many times since we lost the farm. We don't dare touch the compensation money we've been given. We have to save that for school for the children – or for the doctor if we get sick. This is why we came to Garbage Town, for the good money we were told we could earn here.

I think about the 2 fen (100 fen = 1 RMB) we will earn for every cola bottle we find and the 3 fen for every can. With any luck we'll find ten or more today. Maybe we can find something fun for the children while we're at it. Ermao still likes that plastic machine gun I found. But we've got to get out before the garbage trucks arrive.

Although we're all in the same boat, us garbage pickers, there seems to be no solidarity among us. We all want first grabs at the garbage. And when security guards and policemen come to put up the fences to close in the new zone, it will be every man for himself, just like now. Will we ever meet again? I doubt it.

But we're still here, and tomorrow at 4:20 a.m. the train will wake us up again, and we will go on with our scavenging. Where are the jobs? I've been told there are thousands of university graduates who can't find one. So what are the chances for a farmer with no qualifications and no land?

I have heard they built a wall around the new development zone where our farm was. There used to be just fencing, but now they've made it more permanent. Still I dream of returning to my farm. Until it's 4:20 a.m. and the train comes crashing through the house.

Wang Xiao-Shan is Editor-in-Chief of a Chinese newspaper and a well-known cultural critic.

Age 28 · **Occupation** Insurance agent/manager in Beijing · **Family** Single, living with parents · **Home** Living at home in a room in parents' 70 m^2 apartment · **Free time** Exercising, reading newspapers, watching TV, DVDs · **Monthly income (RMB)** Personal – 40,000; Household – n/a · **Household**

LIU YI

Insurance agent
Beijing

budget (RMB) Housing/Utilities – paid by parents; Education – 0; Parent support – 25,000; Health care – n/a; Food/Clothing/Other – 6,000; Savings – 9,000 (in addition, part of "parent support" is, in fact, savings for him, too)

对我来说，主要有四件重要的工作要做，销售、培训、INTERVIEW 和团队经营管理，几乎所有的工作都是围绕这四件事而安排的。以前我全部的时间都用在销售上，随着职位的不断晋升，团队成员的不断扩大，现在更多的时间会放在培训、INTERVIEW 和团队经营管理。晨会之后，我首先要用10分钟左右，听我的助理汇报昨天的工作状况，提醒我们团队内部重要通知，以及今天需要我做的一些事情，例如安排的 INTERVIEW，解决个别团队成员的问题，或参加的会议等，然后我会给助理安排今天需要帮我做的事情，比如打电话据跟安排 INTERVIEW 的时间，联系客户安排见面，以及帮我处理日常的行政事务等。

7:30 – I get up and turn on the TV to watch the news. Working in the financial industry, I've got to keep myself up-to-date all the time. With the news on in the background, I wash my face, brush my teeth, and dress for work.

8:00 – My parents have breakfast ready for me, as usual. Lately I eat whole grain cereal, because it is supposed to be good for you, as well as different kinds of beans and nuts. My parents grind beans each day to make us fresh soy milk. I also have an egg, fried or boiled, with bread, butter, and sausage. It's sort of a half-Chinese, half-Western breakfast.

8:30 – I go down to brush off the dust that has accumulated overnight on my car. Although some efforts have been made, Beijing is still very polluted compared to the coastal cities. In the half hour it takes to get to work, I run into a few minor traffic jams, but I enjoy listening to pop music and entertainment news on the radio. I get there relaxed and ready to start my day.

9:00 – The first thing is our regular morning meeting. In this half-hour, we talk about customers and things like training, promotions, and administrative details. Today, I have organized role-playing to help my team work on some sales techniques. For about five minutes afterwards, we do some physical exercise (stretching, jumping), concluding with some shouting or cheering. This practice seemed very strange to me at first, especially after the sobriety of my old accounting firm. But boldness is something you need in this business, and doing this helps.

9:30 – I meet with my assistant, who preps me for the day and helps me line up my plans for the coming days and weeks.

10:30 – I interview a 39-year-old science Ph.D. with post-doctoral experience. He wants to relocate back to China, like so many people these days. He's interesting, but overqualified. I tell him this, but he's insistent, so I make a snap decision to give him a chance. I explain a couple of sales techniques and ask him to make ten cold calls in the area and be back in one hour with contact details and an insurance history on each. He comes back on time with eight profiles. I call a couple of numbers just to make sure. I'm impressed.

12:00 – I have an hour to myself, while the others are out to lunch. I don't eat lunch because it makes me sleepy afterwards. I usually work on customer files or training material in this time. Sometimes I smoke a cigarette or two to relax.

14:00 – I meet with a potential set of customers – a Chinese-American couple – in a coffee shop, which is a popular place to do business in Beijing. It took me a while to convince them of the value of insurance, but I finally won them over. Insurance is so poorly understood in China. We talk about the pension plan I'm proposing to them and also about their real estate business. They have promised to help me when I want to buy a house one day. In a way, we're friends now, which is a great thing about this job.

16:00 – I hurry back to the office to make a 4 p.m. recruiting interview. The candidate only has a junior college education, but a very strong drive to achieve – probably the most important thing in sales. I arrange for her to attend a training session.

17:30 – I often work until 8 p.m. and then go out to dinner to an area restaurant. My parents eat much earlier, so I don't like to have them bother making an extra meal for me later. Today, I am leaving early because I am meeting a friend for a dinner of Hunan-style bullfrogs. She's in the financial industry, too, and has introduced me to many potential customers. We talk about business and life in general over a delicious, hot, and spicy dinner.

20:30 – I get home, shower, turn on the news, and read the paper. I also flip on the computer and usually go online for news or chats with friends. Sometimes I talk on the telephone, but with the loud speaker on so I can continue doing other things. I like multitasking like this, though my parents think I'm wasting electricity with all these things on. I feel on top of events when I'm like this, and that's key in my business.

24:00 – I switch on "Friends." It's brainless, but funny and I learn a little American slang while I'm at it. The TV turns itself off after the program is over, at which time I am generally sound asleep.

A CHAT WITH LIU YI

How long have you been in the insurance business?
More than five years now. I joined one of the big local accounting firms right after college in 1997 and became an accountant. My mother was an accountant and encouraged me to go in this direction. But after three years or so, I began longing for more independence. Becoming an insurance salesman was appealing because I could be my own boss and could also hopefully earn more money. So I decided to join an insurance company that was just expanding into the Beijing market.

Leaving a secure job to start something entirely different – that was kind of risky, wasn't it?
I knew the industry had great potential for growth and that the competition for jobs there was still not as intense as in most other industries, where you have to have an MBA to even get a foot in the door. I knew my Bachelor's degree in Economics would be enough to sell insurance. Also, many young people here look down on the insurance business, so the field was pretty open. And once I decide to do something, I'm very determined to do it well. As for risk, if you can't take some at my age, when can you? It might be a little late 30 years down the road.

How was it at the beginning?
It was tough. I was earning less and also working very hard. I was either on the phone with clients or visiting them – all day, every day. That's the game of selling insurance. But I never got bored or wondered what it was all for. I'm still working hard, but I have been able to build a team of about 40 agents, so I spend more than half my time on recruiting, training, and managing people. By now, I earn about twice as much as I was earning as a certified accountant.

That's great. What are your plans for the future?
One day I would like to have my own insurance agency. I think this is

a common practice in Canada and other foreign countries. Agents band together and start a firm, just like lawyers and accountants. In the meantime, I'll continue expanding my team at the company. At a certain point, if you're successful enough, you can move into overall management of the business. But right now, I think I would prefer staying out in the field with my team and my clients. You never know what you might feel in the future though, when you're older.

How do you spend your money?
I don't have too many expenses. The biggest is probably my car, but that's primarily for business. So I'm able to give more than half my earnings to my parents, who are retired. They are putting aside most of it in savings for me. That may sound strange for someone my age, but it's the way we've always done things. I guess they still feel responsible for making sure I don't spend my money foolishly. I don't mind that. I'm not in a big hurry to get married or buy a house, so it makes sense to save.

Are your parents putting pressure on you to get married?
Oh, yes. They introduce me to a new candidate practically every day. My colleagues try to fix me up too. I already have a serious relationship with someone, but it's complicated because she is very ill and has been in Japan for treatment for several years now. We see each other when she comes back, but  that's not very often. We text-message each other back and forth when she is up to it. It's very sad, but I still have hope that she'll recover and that we'll get married one day.

What do you feel about China's rapid development?
It's been impressive in terms of infrastructure. It's getting better and better all the time, which of course has a lot to do with the 2008 Olympics.

But as far as the society is concerned, these are crazy times. People are fixated on becoming rich and famous, which probably is normal in a boom period. But there are so many gray areas in the legal system. And opening up the doors so wide to foreign companies, like we have, is also questionable in my mind. Korea made it on its own without foreign joint ventures, and I think we could, too. A good economy is like a good sherry – it takes  time to develop. The way it is, housing prices are going through the ceiling, and the gap between the rich and the poor is getting more and more enormous. Just one indication of this is that we are almost the second largest consumer of luxury goods in the world, but do not produce one single luxury brand. The rich are throwing their money around like there is no tomorrow.

What countries outside of China would you like to visit one day?
I'm not very attracted to the U.S., but Europe interests me quite a bit. These countries seem to have developed a comfortable lifestyle without ruining the environment. The people may not be super rich, but they seem to live well.

So many foreigners are living in China these days. How do you feel about that?
Beijing is an international city now. Foreigners bring new knowledge and perspectives, so they are welcome, as far as I'm concerned. Maybe they will take away jobs, but I am not worried about that personally because I am essentially self-employed.

Are you interested in politics?
I think most of us young Chinese are not very interested in politics per se, but we do have our own ideas. Unlike my parents' generation, we don't blindly accept everything that the government says or does.

Everybody loved the Party back then, and nobody was allowed to say anything bad about it. (My father was even more authoritarian than the government, if that's possible!) I'm actually a member of the Party. I was a student member in high school and then officially joined when I was in college. There is no Party organization in my company that I could report to, so I'm not really active now. And as I see more of the dark side of society come to light, I do seriously wonder about many of the Party's reforms. Medical reform, for one, has been a nearly complete failure, as most people by now recognize.

THE SHOPKEEPER'S TALE
by YiYi

I am going to tell you what it is to be happy. My name is Wang Xiaohua, I am married to Li Daming, and we have a son, Xiaoming. Our hometown is in Hebei province. There we had some old cattle and some land that couldn't produce anything good. So we came to the city. We brought our son, who was still in primary school, along with us. My 80-year-old mother stayed behind.

Others who had come to the city from our hometown found jobs as manual laborers. They told us of the long hours, the hard work, and the low wages – hardly enough to keep body and soul together. So Daming and I decided on another course, to open a little shop selling household supplies.

We soon found a small but suitable space for our shop and also a room nearby where we could live. The shop was truly small, but, as the Chinese proverb goes, a sparrow may be small, but it has everything it needs to live. Actually, you'd be amazed at how much we have managed to pack into this space. We sell everything from thread to oil, salt, soy sauce, vinegar, and more. After three years, we are doing very well with it. People around here come in regularly because we are convenient but not expensive. We have already paid back everything we borrowed to set ourselves up, and we can now afford to send Xiaoming to the local school. We can even afford to send a little money home to our families every month.

On this late September day, Daming is up before 6 a.m. and soon on his way to our suppliers. He makes this trip on his three-wheeled bike once a month. I get up, too. After washing up and dressing, I put a pot of millet porridge on the stove and yesterday's dirty clothes into the wash. I then dash over to the shop to receive the early deliveries.

By the time I get back, it is 6:30 a.m., so I wake up a sleepy Xiaoming. We have breakfast together and then I see him off to school, having first made sure that he has everything he should in his school bag. I take the meal I cooked last night and hurry to the shop. When I get there and open up, Aunt Zhao asks for a couple grams of brown sugar and some eggs. She says that her daughter-in-law has just had a baby and needs to build up her strength.

As she is leaving, several other aunts and uncles from the neighborhood walk in. (We call our elders that as a sign of respect.) Most of them have just gotten back from taking their grandchildren to kindergarten or school. They like to stop by here afterwards to chat. Their children are all at work, so they have no one to talk to at home. I don't mind, though, because business is slack in the early morning. And, if the truth be told, it's company for me and I get to keep up with what's going on in the neighborhood.

Not long after all the aunts and uncles have left – it must have been 10 a.m. – Daming comes back with his bike piled high with supplies. He looks hot and exhausted, so I give him a glass of water. Together we start unloading the goods and putting them away. We finish about noon. Xiaoming gets his meal at school, so Daming and I eat together in the back of the shop. I warm up the food I brought from home— fried eggs with chives, stewed apples, and beans. Daming didn't get breakfast this morning, so I let him have some of mine. Afterwards, I tell him he should take a little nap, which he does. We don't get many customers in the afternoon, two or three at the most.

Today, there's the man who always comes in to make a phone call, as well as a young mother looking for shampoo and another one wanting some perfumed soap. When people start coming home from their jobs at the end of the day, that's when business really picks up. Then they drop by for rice and other things for dinner, and soon we are enveloped in the mouth-watering fragrance of other people's dinners being prepared nearby.

Xiaoming comes in about this time from school, which is not far away. We are glad we can let him come and go on his own without worrying. We make the usual little space for him on the counter so that he can do his homework. And to tide him over till we get home, I let him have a couple of cookies. I am concerned that he's not getting enough of the right food when he gets snacks like that. But I console myself that he will have a good supper with us later and has had a good midday meal at school.

The streetlights come on while we are at our busiest in the shop. These streetlights, funnily enough, contribute something to my happiness each evening. Once the shop is locked up and we start walking home – my husband beside me and my son's hand in mine – each streetlight casts our shadow before us. First it's short and then it gets longer and longer until it finally disappears. Then we're at the next streetlight and the pattern repeats itself. Observing our three ever-lengthening shadows, I feel happy.

Of course, we must pay our rent at the end of the month, save for our son's education, and send money to our families. Of course, we will work hard and have time for little else. But we are healthy, if not wealthy. And we know there is nothing more valuable than the love we have together. So I look down at the short and the long, the near and the far shadows of the three of us, and I feel joy welling up in me.

YiYi, whose name is otherwise Gong Jia, works in the financial world, but has a passion for writing. She is the author of many published stories.

Age 78 · **Occupation** Retired professor of political science in Beijing · **Family** Wife, 43-year-old son · **Home** Three-bedroom condominium · **Free time** Bowling, reading, surfing the internet, watching TV · **Monthly income (RMB)**

WANG YUNKUN

Retired professor of political science
Beijing

Personal (pension) 2,500; Household – 3,500 · **Household budget (RMB)**
Housing/Utilities – 500; Education – 0; Health care – 300; Food/Clothing/
Other – 2,000; Savings – 700

早晨按习惯4点醒来，躺在床上回忆新年节日期间在电视屏幕看的去年贺岁片"天下无贼"，剧情编的有新意，~~New year film~~ 赏析主题思想是宣扬中国文化"人性善"的理论。女贼同情一个淳朴的小青年，认为要保护他携带的6万元打工钱不被另一派黑道上的窃贼偷去，和其男友准备行侠仗义的故事。为了弄清楚人性善与人性恶的两个相反根源，5点我起床打开网页查看Google引出的论述。中国人以传统文化观念习惯认为恰相反，占西方文化中统治地位的一个主流思想应是"性恶论"。西方宗教之比中"原罪"original sin是观念核心，人生来就是有罪的。性恶论在社会和政治理论中的体现，就是对法制的重视。马克思主义信仰无神论，不相信原罪说，所以马克思主义也相信"性善论"，认为人的本性是好的，公平的，善的。只是私有制出现后，阶级和国家出现，社会变坏了。马克思说要回到共产主义，那种私有制和阶级出现以前的平等社会。

　　孟子提出性善论，孟子把天作为善的根源，则认为人的性善植根于天的道德属性，沟通了人的心灵和形上的天，使性善获得终极的根据。　　　　试观今日中国社会，改革开放以来，经济迅猛发展，冲垮了传统的中国文化，使人性善的观念大打折扣。社会上物欲横流尔虞我诈，人人为了天诛地灭。哪儿再看到雷锋式人物的踪影。特权阶级，高层人物，毛泽东的政策把中国推到崩溃边缘，以致网上自由论坛把他"掘墓鞭尸"以向中国人民谢罪的说法。

我是那董智教的信仰者，但我的身受经验使我认为"人性恶"的理论是普遍可见的。共产主义给一些人性恶的物种披上了一层革命，掩饰了其凶狠的本性。就此而言，我受到一个退休的共产党员的同僚的人身攻击。在职时，和潘某人素无交往，退休后近二年，以（墨翻译）他（墨翻译）收入颇丰，请我在大饭馆中吃饭多次。最后终笑 这么投机准出意，

我鄙视了他邀请我全家去他新居豪宴以约谈。他怀着感恩，居然我个党外群众仍想揶斥他的邀请，于是他在网上撰文选了个大题目"东方与西方误"，对我诬蔑造谣进行人身攻击，终于他暴露出他已过70岁的人，罢不掉着想到的以外衣的恶人，什么"三个代表""和谐社会"。由他这个貌似君子的老人是个天生的恶人。他本那政治学者出身，翻译是他的用他的小技，随着收入多了，的君子

腰缠万贯（他自称月入5位数）目空一切了，散布谎言

For a congenial friend a thousand
toasts are two few, in a disagreeble conversation one word
more is too many.

Wang Yunkun's Diary

4:00 – I woke up, as usual, about this time. Lying in bed, I reflected on a film I'd seen on TV over the New Year's holiday: "A World without Thieves," which draws its theme from the traditional Chinese belief in man's innocence, or the concept that human beings are by nature good. In it, a female thief runs into a naive young man with 60,000 yuan in his pocket. She feels sorry for him, so she and her boyfriend, also a thief, fight to protect him from a gang of other thieves.

5:00 – Curious about the overall theme of original sin, as opposed to innocence, I got up and googled it.

6:00 – I drank a cup of milk with instant coffee.

6:30 – I listened to the English Studio Classroom program on the radio, as I've been doing every day for the last three years or so. I'm trying to keep mentally active, so I won't get debilitated by something like Alzheimer's. When I hear new words on the program, which I often do, I look them up in the dictionary.

9:00 – I went to a little shop for a bowl of wonton soup. It's a very popular, traditional place with excellent food. I watched through the window as a woman made the wontons – 40 a minute! With a snack bar like this, you can earn enough to support a family and afford a comfortable life in this city. Back in the 1950s, a bowl of wonton soup cost 10 fen (100 fen = 1 yuan), which was 1/875th of my salary. Now, a bowl costs 4 yuan, which is 1/584th of my pension.

10:00 – I arrived at the bowling alley and played six games. My best score was 139, and my average was 113 (out of 300). I'm the oldest player in our group, and a score of 200 points is rare even for younger, skilled players. Bowling is good for my health. It also helps keep my thinking sharp. I have become addicted to this game. But how long will I be able to play?

12:00 – I stop by home briefly, then go to a nearby place for noodles with fried brown sauce, a very simple lunch. Sometimes, I go to the western-style Kiessling restaurant in the city center for a change. My favorite dishes are creamy mushroom soup, pork steak, and braised beef with potato salad, which costs around 30 yuan.

17:30 – I turn on CCTV's "Legal Matters Online," a Chinese version of Sherlock Holmes, which I never miss. Following their deductive reasoning has gradually improved my skills, I feel. The program also makes you curious about the legal system here.

18:30 – We had prepared some special food for a traditional Chinese festival, which was today, but since we had left-over braised beef with potato salad, we decided to eat the delicacies tomorrow. I savored a bit of American whiskey to pay tribute to the festival. I recall that tomorrow I have my twice weekly foot massage, which has helped me with my insomnia. I can now sleep for six hours every night, though I may still wake up twice during the night.

A CHAT WITH WANG YUNKUN

Where did you go to college?
I graduated from Beijing University in 1952 after nine months working on a land reform project in Guangxi. The Party wanted all young students to take part in the class struggle. That was Mao's theory.

What did you do after graduation?
Party officials didn't consider me eligible for a good job in Beijing because I came from a family of higher ranking clerks. They wanted young men from peasant and worker families, so I was assigned to teach Russian in Hebei near Beijing. At that time, the Party leaned toward Russia, so English was out  of favor. Later, in the Khrushchev years, Russian fell out of favor, and I was sent back to Beijing to teach English at a middle school.

I understand you have a degree from a U.S. university.
Yes. When Deng Xiaoping took the reins and began to promote openness, I decided to be bold and enrolled at the University of California at Berkeley. This was paid for by the Chinese government. I got my Master's degree in political science in 1983 at the age of 55. I then returned and worked at the Chinese Academy of Social Sciences and also served as Secretary General of the Chinese Association of Political Science. In 1989, I received a Fulbright scholarship and spent a year lecturing at North Carolina State University. Over the years, I attended International Political Science Association conferences around the world, and have lectured at many U.S. universities.

Do you think people in the west know much about Chinese culture?
As for Americans, most know next to nothing. They don't even know where Beijing is. But there are a few Western scholars who have a very thorough understanding of Chinese history and literature.

Where is your wife from?

Her family is from North Korea, though she's never been there. She was born in Harbin and brought up by her uncle because her parents died very young. In the 1960s, her uncles went back to North Korea. She sends them money regularly for food and clothing.

How did you and your wife meet?

I met her around 1960. She is my second wife. My first wife and I got divorced, and my younger daughter stayed with me. Later on, my first wife took our two daughters to the U.S., where they still live. I have no direct contact with them these days. One works for an IT company in Dallas. The other deals cards in a Seattle casino.

You also have a son, I understand. How is he doing?

He's unemployed right now. I was very angry at the Academy for laying him off. He occasionally sells for Amway, the American company, but he needs something full time. He is 43 and can't get married because of his health problems. Every year, he has one or two strokes.

How was it for you during the Cultural Revolution?

It was the worst time of my life. Also, my son was very young and not healthy. In the summer of 1966, the Red Guards searched and sealed  my house, and I was taken into custody for ten days. Some of my relatives had reported me to the Red Guards saying I had a pistol. When they found no evidence of weapons, they released me. My mother was in Hong Kong at the time and didn't dare to come back. My brother in Michigan got an immigration visa for her.

What effect did the Cultural Revolution have on your work?

As a middle school teacher, I went with my students every semester to

the country for political training. The authorities didn't bother me any
more because they had no evidence, but I was very depressed.
Students weren't interested in learning,
especially not a foreign language, and I
was not allowed to attend certain kinds
of meetings or even to go to Tiananmen
Square. I was also discriminated against
because I had relatives in the U.S. The
school administration decided all that, with the help of worker
propaganda teams and the Red Guards. They had that kind of power.

How did it change you personally?
The traditional Chinese view is that human nature is good, but I don't
believe in that anymore. This is similar to the Marxist view – that it is
only after the emergence of private ownership that social classes
appear and humans become evil. I feel now human beings are
inherently bad, that they are born with original sin.

Your house was taken away and then returned. When was that?
We finally got it back in 1983. It was Deng Xiaoping's policy to return
private homes to their owners. Fearing another Cultural Revolution,
though, I donated ten big rooms to the Housing Bureau. We kept nine
rooms for ourselves, divided up among three families.

What do you feel are China's greatest developmental challenges?
Corruption is a big issue, even within the Academy. A web news report
I saw exposed some of the dark sides of this society, things that
 newspapers don't write about.
Corruption is an especially big problem
in the provinces. I just saw a report about
51 bankers in the provinces who
embezzled money and fled. They have
been granted asylum in foreign countries

and probably won't be brought back because of the death penalty here.

What do you think of the Taiwan issue?

I am in favor of peaceful reunification. When former KMT chief Lian Zhan came to Beijing in 2005, he was welcomed warmly. The new KMT head Ma Yingjiu and Lian Zhan have formed a new front, so there is some hope.

What do you think of the medical system?

Within the Academy, it's no problem. I am reimbursed for up to 90 percent of my medical expenses and can file claims at any time.

How was your experience at the Academy?

Sometimes I think a few of the leaders were envious because of my frequent invitations to lecture at American universities. I was sometimes called pro-American, meaning under their control.

You were in Beijing when the Tiananmen incident took place?

Yes. Since then, people have gained more freedom of expression, at least on the Internet, though they're not allowed to express hostility toward the government. But intellectuals in China have changed in the meantime. Most are more concerned about making more money than changing the world. Some are probably in despair because they know that the nature of the regime hasn't really changed. There still is no freedom of speech here.

THE GAS STATION ATTENDANT'S TALE
by Old Cat

In China, "refueling" has a double meaning. It means filling up your car, of course, but it also means, in a metaphorical sense, inspiring others to achieve their best. You could say that both capture the essence of life in contemporary China.

In Beijing, be it on the city beltways or on the bigger highways, gas stations are everywhere. The busiest people at these stations are the uniformed attendants, many of whom have a uniform expression as well. There's a kind of helpless perplexity to be seen in their eyes, perhaps a question forming behind them: How did I end up in this job?

Not all are puzzled, however. On this September morning, Beijing is bursting with activity, as it is wont to be. On the outer beltway, traffic has come to a crawl because of an accident. But this is unimportant to Xiaofeng, who is 22 and an expert at negotiating through traffic on his bike.

Leaning his bike against the railing in a corner, he goes in to relieve a fellow worker who has been on the night shift. For a gas station attendant, shift handover means, more or less, a handover of the oil can. There is nothing else — no information — that needs to be passed along. As it was on the night shift, so it will be on the day shift, repetition of a nearly identical process on only slightly different cars, one after the other.

On his arrival at the station, Xiaofeng saw that prices still had not been reduced at his station, despite the drop on the international markets over a month ago. This means that people will be giving him grief again about the pump price, as if it were his fault. (This might also contribute to the helpless perplexity of attendants, if you think about it.)

Dreading the moans and maybe the curses, Xiaofeng stays as long as he can at the window of the station's store. He kills time reading up on the various foods and drinks offered inside. As slowly as he can, he lifts the last piece of steamed bun towards his mouth. Not until the hands of the clock point exactly to 6:50 does he put on his gloves, take out the rags he had stuck into his belt, and head toward the pumps.

Xiaofeng shares a one-story dormitory with friends who were at polytechnic school with him. The house is far out, outside of the fifth beltway, which is why it takes him 40 minutes to get to work. Despite everything, he is happy to have this job.

When Xiaofeng left his hometown in Inner Mongolia to come to Beijing, he knew his school record would make it impossible to land him a job in an office. So he was pleased when, after working as a courier for only two months, the employment agency sent him to this gas station.

During training, which consisted of cleaning cars, his salary was only 750 yuan a month. Once he became good enough to clean the whole exterior during refueling, he became a "regular worker" earning 900 yuan a month. Like the others, he was then able to supplement his wages by selling car accessories and products to drivers.

Just before noon, when there are fewer cars coming in, Xiaofeng takes his lunch box and hunkers down on the steps with his workmates. The heady smell of the gasoline doesn't dampen his appetite; to the contrary, it reminds him how grateful he is to the station for providing him with his lunch, small though it is. While he eats today, he also chats with the cashier, who is hardly more than a girl.

After lunch, he has enough time to jump over the railing and hide in the corner for a smoke. He also turns on his secondhand mobile and sends a text message to his girlfriend in Inner Mongolia. He isn't allowed to make mobile phone calls from the station, and smoking is most definitely not allowed. As a result, he saves a lot of money on cigarettes and phone calls.

Nonetheless, lunch ends far too soon. Even before he has a chance to gulp down some of the purified water that is also one of his perks, he has to fill up a car that has just come in. The driver is a pretty girl, at least in Xiaofeng's eyes. "How much do you want?" Xiaofeng asks. "A 100 yuan, please!" she says. So Xiaofeng sets the refueling gauge and runs over to the cashier with the money. Bringing back the receipt, he grabs the free newspaper and gives it to her, as he does with all his customers. As the girl drives off, he stands for a moment watching her. In the midst of a reverie, he hears a whistle and feels a rag hit his head.

In the afternoon after shift handover, the pay clerk gives him his wages. In salaries and commissions, he has earned a little over 1,000 yuan this month. Seeing this, he quickly makes a plan to buy a 50-yuan rechargeable card for his mobile, pick up one of the free newspapers left, and bike back to his dorm. But first he will take a shower at the station and put on the T-shirt given to him by a tire company.

Tonight in Beijing, in a busy lane outside the fifth beltway, Xiaofeng will leave his dorm and go with friends for a happy-hour drink. While his friends will probably go on to a nearby club for entertainment of a kind he does not choose, Xiaofeng will find a phone booth to take a call from his girlfriend. Then he will go back to his house and watch TV. When he is tired, he will climb into his upper bunk and within moments be sound asleep. In the morning he will again ride his bike to the gas station.

When he has saved enough money, Xiaofeng will go back to his hometown in Inner Mongolia and marry his girlfriend. Maybe then they will both come back and work at the station, refueling cars side by side. One of his dreams is to have his own gas station. He admits to himself, despite all his optimism, that this dream is many years away.

Old Cat, whose real name is Si Xinying, is a columnist for several newspapers and magazines. His published works include the novels "Cherish the Sunlight" and "Malicious Happiness" as well as textbooks on marketing and strategy.

Age 30 · **Occupation** Bank manager in Beijing · **Family** Single, living with parents · **Home** 150 m², three-bedroom apartment · **Free time** Reading, watching foreign DVD movies · **Monthly income (RMB)** Personal – 14,000;

Liu Weina

Bank manager
Beijing

Household – n/a · **Household budget (RMB)** Housing/Utilities – 0 (paid by parents); Parent support – 0; Health care – n/a; Food/Clothing/Other – 3,500; Savings – 10,500

Liu Weina's Diary

6:00 – The alarm clock rang for the first time.

6:15 – It rang a second time, and I got up. It was still dark outside.

6:50 – Ate breakfast – two pieces of bread and a glass of soy milk.

7:15 – Left in the darkness for work.

8:10 – Arrived at work. It was fairly fast this morning, not many traffic jams. I listened to China Radio International on the way, as usual. At my desk, I switched on my computer and checked my e-mail.

8:30 – The bank opened. I picked up where I had left off on writing about on-line banking.

9:45 – Nearly finished my piece on on-line banking; had only one rate inquiry left; started rethinking the deposit/withdrawal business process.

9:48 – Went to Finance & Accounting to search for documents.

9:52 – Went to the assistant general manager (GM) to discuss and ask for instructions about business regulations.

10:05 – Back to my office to write.

11:45 – Completed the business process for deposits and withdrawals and passed it on to the assistant GM for review.

11:47 – Logged on to sina.com to read the news.

12:18 – Had lunch at McDonald's with two colleagues.

12:40 – Returned to the office to surf the Internet.

13:00 – Contacted the Ministry of Science & Technology to confirm changes and progress in business demand.

13:13 – Began work on revising the manual on internal controls.

13:40 – Issued certificates of deposit (CD) to a customer.

14:30 – Released notice announcing CDs online.

15:00 – Sent off some documents.

15:30 – Drafted statements for CDs.

16:30 – Revised detailed rules for reporting losses.

16:40 – Answered questions for an important customer about CDs.

17:00 – Discussed business with the assistant GM.

17:38 – Left the office.

18:50 – Arrived home.

19:00 – Had supper with mom and dad. My mom made dumplings and some vegetable and tofu dishes.

19:30 – Watched television in my own room – an American comedy on HBO. My parents watched CCTV news in the living room.

20:30 – Went to the gym.

22:00 – Returned home and went to bed an hour later.

A CHAT WITH LIU WEINA

What is your bank's major area of business and your role?
Our bank was similar to a rural credit cooperative, but it's now a legally incorporated entity. It is one of 15 corporations of this kind in Beijing. We offer banking services, but are not permitted to get involved with investments or stock trading. I joined the bank in August and am in retail banking. I graduated from university in 1997, worked for five years at the China Construction Bank (CCB), and then left in 2002 to study in Australia.

Where did you study in Australia?
In Sydney. It's nice there. I stayed for over a year.

How did you decide what to study when you went abroad?
My contract at CCB was complete. Lots of people leave at the end of their contracts, which are either three or five years long. Having already worked in banking, I felt this was a good business to be in, so I wanted to study something in that field. I had read about the financial investments program there and thought it would be right for me, so that's what I chose.

Tuition is quite high in Australia, isn't it?
It was nearly 30,000 Australian dollars, and living expenses came to about 20,000. But it wasn't difficult to get in. As far as entrance exams went, you only needed to take an English language skills test. I had saved for five years while I was working, but that would only have covered living expenses. My parents helped me with the rest.

How did you find this job after your return?
I heard about it from a friend. The bank had been looking for people with a background in commercial banking, like me. I hoped there would be more opportunities there than at the bigger banks, which had just finished their spring recruiting. I also didn't want to work again in one of those big organizations, with thousands of employees. There are

only about 200 professional jobs in our bank, so there should be better opportunities here than in bigger banks.

Did your classmates coming back from Australia have the same luck?
They all found good jobs too. All had at least three years of work experience before they went to Australia, which was the minimum requirement for acceptance to our program. One is doing asset analysis at New China Life Insurance, another is working in investments in Shanghai, and another is working at the Bank of China in Jinzhou. Two classmates have positions with foreign banks.

Did you ever think about staying in Australia?
My thought was, if it's good, I'll stay, but if it's only so-so, I'll come back.

 In the end, I decided there was not enough going on in Australia. People earn 30,000 to 40,000 Australian dollars a year and seem happy with that. There's a kind of complacency, I guess. But in China, people are very motivated to earn more. The country is not that stable yet, but this isn't a bad thing. It means that if you work hard and have some luck, you can reach middle management when you're in your early 30s. In Australia, it's more like in your 40s.

Does your job meet your expectations?
I thought at first it would be very strenuous. But it's actually not bad at all. The workload is not that heavy. And my income is commensurate with it. So it's good for me. I don't want to be tired all the time.

Are you living with your parents now?
Yes. My dad is still working, but my mom retired a long time ago. My dad is in the telecommunications business.

Do you have plans to buy a car or an apartment?

If I bought an apartment, I would want one right in the city. But I'm in no rush to do that. I don't have any plans to get married right now, so I'll stay at my parents'. Most young people whose parents live in the same city do the same, at least until they get married. And if they do buy an apartment, they buy one close by. I don't need a car.

What do you do on holidays?

My father rarely has vacation, so when we go somewhere, it's mostly to someplace nearby. I don't travel much on my own, although I do have five days of paid vacation.

Do you watch TV or go to movies?

Not very often. I occasionally buy Chinese or western DVDs. I like the new releases from America, and I also like HBO, which is provided by our community. National Geographic and Phoenix are also my favorite channels. I usually don't watch the domestic ones.

Do you read books, newspapers, or magazines?

I read financial and other news on the Internet, and I enjoy reading a novel now and then. Right now, I'm reading a "Harry Potter" book in  the original, and I have bought "The Da Vinci Code," also in the original. I always prefer English editions if they're available. I also read Chinese novels, but not often. I enjoy books about ancient Chinese culture and literature, like poems from the Tang Dynasty and lyrics from the Song Dynasty. I have electronic versions of these books, but it can be tiring reading them on a screen, so I more often read "real" books.

What are your impressions of countries outside China?

Well, Europe seems to be quite a lot like Australia. They're both mature, though the standard of living in Europe is generally higher, I believe. Many of my classmates who went to Europe or Australia came back with the attitude that work is necessary but a good life is more important. Those who went to America tended not to think that way. New York, especially, is pretty chaotic. Everyone is always in a hurry. Beijing is like that now too – so many people, so many cars. But unlike China, all of them generally have very good social welfare systems.

What makes you think that?
People get unemployment compensation and social security. In Australia almost everything is covered. Their institutions for the elderly are also good. Here it's very different. If you get sick, you never know how much it's going to cost you. That's why the Chinese are so keen on saving. No matter what the government does to reduce interest rates on savings, having money in the bank makes people feel secure. Even when the stock market is up, savings account deposits don't go down.

How do you view China's development?
I think the biggest challenge is its extremes. The rich are very rich, and the poor are very poor. It is not so bad in Beijing proper, but in the outskirts, some people don't even have water. Morality and ethics could be improved as well. Corruption is a problem from top to bottom in both large and small organizations, even in banks.

You have a good job, good health, and a good education. Do you have any worries at all?
I am concerned about the future – about how far I can go in this job. If there is no more room for advancement, I'll have to change jobs.

What about social security, welfare, insurance?
I don't have any now, but I might consider it. The insurance industry used to be poorly regulated, but it's better now. And there are also foreign companies in the market now. I might choose one of them one day.

Age 29 · **Occupation** Professional singer in Beijing/Tibet/Taiwan · **Family** Husband · **Home** Three-story house in Beijing suburbs · **Free time** Meditating, reading, writing, singing, dancing

YANGJIN LAMU

Professional singer
Beijing/Tibet/Taiwan

Other personal information not provided

YANGJIN LAMU'S DIARY

5:00 – I woke up, got dressed, and walked to the temple of the Bodhisattva Guanyin, the Goddess of Mercy. Refreshed and restored, I went to say my morning prayers. In my prayers, I softly read aloud some treasured Tibetan songs, and with the holy chant of "OM Mani Padme Hum" I prayed for happiness for all living creatures and their deliverance from suffering.

6:00 – After my prayers, I went back to the monastery, where one of the old monks, always smiling, had prepared a delicious but simple vegetarian breakfast for me. He also gave me some aloe he had picked and said its juice would make me beautiful.

7:30 – The nun in charge of the grounds asked me to rake all of the leaves around the monastery, which covered half the mountain. I agreed, but I began to wonder how I could possibly do this and still have time to accomplish my purpose – to record music in these gorgeous surroundings. As I worked, I recalled my mother's advice to take advantage of physical labor as a way of practicing focus. I began to hear my mother's voice, then the chirping of birds, the humming of insects, the rustling of leaves and soon I had not only cleared away all the leaves but also the petty thoughts in my mind.

10:30 – After showering in my room, I went back to the temple and with prayers, lit incense and a lamp in the Bodhisattva Guanyin's honor. Seeing dust and cobwebs on the sacred sandalwood statue above me, I began cleaning it, without really thinking, then with a kind of elation, sensing that the Bodhisattva was accepting my ministrations. I then cleaned the temple floor. As I stood in the calm of the gleaming surfaces around us, I was brought a plate of cut fruits sent by the nun who had asked my help. I was touched by her gesture.

11:30 – After freshening up, I went to the dining hall, where the monks serve hundreds of local people every day, in addition to their own.

I asked to visit the kitchen afterwards and there met the monk who had cooked for us. My mother told me that the quality of the food can be seen in the cleanliness of the kitchen.

12:30 – Lying on the simple, hard bed in my room and listening to nature's melodies outside my open window, I slipped into a deep sleep.

15:00 – My recording crew and musicians arrived – four in all. We started walking around looking for the right place to record. I decided that the Bodhisattva Guanyin temple, where I had spent the early morning hours, would be the best. I prayed for her blessing to record music in her temple, to allow us to be instruments of her wisdom and joy. Assured of the answer, I let the crew set up their equipment. I began to sing at some point, and they slowly caught up with the song. Cicadas started making a terrible racket outside, though, forcing us to wait patiently for quite a long time. Finally, they let us play without interruption, and we worked into the night. Although not Buddhist, like me, my group seemed to be drawn into the peace and harmony of the temple and the sacred songs I was singing.

24:00 – We went outside for a rest. Looking up at the moon in its serenity, I heard in my mind the words of a Buddhist song written by the Sixth Dalai Lama about the moon, which he compared to the glowing face of a young girl. Then I heard a melody in my mind that seemed to carry the words. We immediately recorded the song. It was the only love song in my album. When we ended the session, I felt so grateful for the forces that had brought me and these people together in this place.

A CHAT WITH YANGJIN LAMU

Where did you grow up?

I come from a small town on the border of Tibet and Qinghai province. As children, we herded yaks and sheep, and people there still live very simply and close to nature.

Tell me a little about your mother, who had such a strong influence in your life.

My mother was illiterate but so full of wisdom and love. She guided me in Buddhist ways, but never preached. Some of Buddha's teachings that she shared with me − like returning good for evil − were harder to understand as a child, but I came to realize the beauty of such acts as I grew older.

How did you end up becoming a professional musician?

Living in the rugged mountains of Tibet, watching over the yaks or the sheep as they grazed, I would sing to keep myself company out in the meadows. I got the nickname "Meadow Lark" after a while. My mother liked to sing, too, and sang to us as babies and also when she did her work. So it is a part of my heritage. Later, I became a music teacher in our middle school and then got admitted  to the university to study music. My sisters and I have also sung and danced together professionally. These days, in my work to foster understanding of the Tibetan culture, singing is my most important channel of communication. Singing now in temples and in nature as I do, I feel I have found my true self. I don't know whether that is being a musician or not, but I do know that music never leaves me.

At one time you were more of a business entrepreneur. How was that?

In Beijing, already in my first year of university, I became disillusioned with higher education in China. It was an atmosphere foreign to me. Students seemed to think more about entertainment than education.

I was seriously considering following my childhood dream of becoming a Buddhist nun, when I ran into a friend of my sister, who wanted to start a business selling Tibetan natural medicines. Intrigued and eager to get back to Tibet, I founded a business with her. I worked in it for more than five years, but over time, I began to feel dissatisfied and again had thoughts of becoming a nun. This time I met my future husband!

How did you meet him?

He was running a small school in Zhongshan in Guangdong province, and I was part of a delegation from Tibet that visited it. Not long after, he came to Tibet, and he asked to speak to me before the program

 started. After chatting for a while, he suddenly asked me to marry him. I was stunned, of course. I barely knew him and vaguely heard that he was from a prestigious family in Taiwan. Over the following months, he phoned me often, and I gradually started to consider it. With our Buddhist faith as a bond, I thought, perhaps we could work together to spread greater understanding about Tibet. Then fate stepped in. We had the honor to meet the head of the Kagyu sect, His Holiness the 17th Karmapa, Ogyen Trinley Dorje, under whom my future brother-in-law was studying. He asked the Karmapa whether his brother should marry me. He gave his answer the next day: "Marry in May." So we did – and we are very happy.

Tell me something about your music.

I don't work in a studio to make my music, but in Buddhist temples or in natural surroundings. The lyrics are all from Tibetan poems written thousands of years ago by enlightened sages. I also incorporate many Bodhisattva chants. These are the languages of the cosmos and contain special energy in themselves. I serve only as a conduit for these holy sounds. As for the melodies I sing, they come to me on their own. I cannot call them my creation. In fact, being full of ideas at the start of a work session tends to block me. The best ideas flow when I am simply open to receiving them.

Could you tell me more about your religion?
Buddhism is not really a religion in the classic sense because it does not teach the worship of an external god. It tells us instead how to develop wisdom and compassion, how to become the masters of our lives. Buddhist doctrine explains the true existence of cause and effect, and it teaches that we must journey through the six realms of reincarnation, whether we choose to or not.

You spend much time in Taiwan as well as in mainland China. What is the biggest difference between the two?
In Taiwan, you can see the roots of ancient Chinese culture everywhere you look. There are many temples and many monks willing to help you

 with your troubles. People are, on the whole, good and honest, in my perception. And they are very creative. Every little shop you see is a work of art. They are also eager to learn and grow. Many, many people go to night school to enhance their lives. It's part of the culture. In mainland China, however, the focus is more on economic development, which is understandable given the huge gap between the rich and the poor. This is China's most important challenge, I think, but overcoming it may not happen easily. The disaster of the Cultural Revolution undermined people's basic orientation in life. It robbed them of their values and their faith.

How do you view the world outside China?
I haven't traveled much outside China, so my knowledge is limited.

I think the U.S. has performed an amazing feat to become the biggest world power in just 200 years. But I have the impression that many people there are not really happy, despite their material wealth. I feel there is little understanding of the profound meaning of human life.

About the Japanese, I admire their precision and earnestness, but sometimes I feel they are just too serious. As for South Koreans, I see them investing much in educating themselves and teaching their children right from wrong. I am also impressed by their spirit of unity, like how people donated money, jewelry, and other valuables to help the country out of its financial crisis. Even better, in my mind, would be if every country would extend selfless caring beyond their borders, throughout the world!

Age 31 · **Occupation** Restaurant worker in Shanghai · **Family** Husband, six-year-old daughter · **Home** 30 m², one-bedroom apartment shared with another family · **Free time** Watching educational TV, helping daughter with homework · **Monthly income (RMB)** Personal – 600; Household – 3,000 ·

WANG XI

Migrant restaurant worker
Shanghai

Household budget (RMB) Housing/Utilities – 600; Education – 450; Parent support – 200; Health care – nothing this year, but has been as high as 6,000 in a year; Food/Clothing/Other – 500; Savings – 1,250

11月16号 星期三 天气阴

"妈妈，我要起床了。"随着宝宝的声音，睁开眼一看是早上7点钟，坐起来让你自己穿，宝宝穿上紫色的带小兔和白色的毛衣。我也起床在穿的睡衣上套了一件马夹穿好拖鞋和宝宝一起到卫生间洗刷，我边帮宝宝刷牙边听音乐，一边问今天早餐吃什么，宝宝想有妈妈自己包的馄饨、面条、还有蛋炒饭，宝宝选了吃蛋炒饭，宝宝自己洗，我到厨房为她做饭。我先洗好锅 再从冰箱里拿出鸡蛋和米饭，打鸡蛋打好放在碗里放少许的盐调好，把锅点好，放点油过一分钟再把调好的鸡蛋放在锅里翻炒1分钟再放米饭，再翻炒两分钟就放点味精少许的盐，葱，起锅。这样一碗香喷喷的蛋炒饭就炒好了，这时宝宝也洗刷好了，宝宝走到桌边闻了闻说妈妈做的饭真香，我听了很开心，说"那你就多吃点吧"。我看宝宝吃得香，我也要到卫生间去洗刷，几分钟后老公也起床了，我也洗好了，在脸上擦点香，平时我很不化妆的，可擦霜还是必须的。我把今天早上要洗的衣服收到一起放在卫生间，再给梳子。这时宝宝也吃好了，擦干净嘴巴走过来说："妈妈帮我梳头"，我跟她扎了一个小辫子，两边各夹了一个小白兔的发夹。（宝宝今年满6岁，属兔的，所以喜欢小白兔的饰品）宝宝自己穿我为她准备好的衣服，裤子，外套是粉红色的休闲服，配了一条牛仔裤和一双运动鞋。宝宝的皮肤很白，而且还有一个小酒窝，很可爱的。这时，老公也洗刷好了，换上衣服送宝宝上幼儿园，幼儿园离家很近5分钟就到了。当时已经7点50分了，宝宝跟我再见，说："妈妈，下班早点接我。"等宝宝走后，我开始洗衣，用两个盆各放半盆热水，两勺洗衣粉，浅色的放一个盆，深色的放一个盆，我先洗浅色的一盆，浅色的不是很脏，所以洗起来很快，这时，老公送完女儿已经回来了，说帮我一起洗，一会儿就洗好了，老公晾衣服，我用洗过衣服的水拖地，我们借租的房子是一室一厅，所以很快拖洗干净了，一看时间快8点半了，回家看见镜子整一整，我换上了昨晚准备好的衣服，裤子，出门了，老公把门锁好，我挽着老公的手出门了。我们在离家一个饭店上班的，而且都是骑自行车，我们是9:00上班，从家里到饭店需要骑20分钟的车，要经过6个红绿灯，每次老公总让我骑在他的前面，这样他说会放心。我们说说笑笑一会

WANG XI'S DIARY

7:00 – My daughter, Baobao, woke me up. After we washed ourselves and brushed our teeth, I asked what she would like for breakfast. She chose egg fried rice. My husband then got up. I finished dressing and put some scented lotion on my face. Baobao asked me to comb her hair. I made a little ponytail and put a rabbit clip on each side. (Baobao was born in the Year of the Rabbit, so she loves things like that.) She then put on the clothes I had set out for her the night before – a pink sweater, a pair of jeans, and sneakers. After my husband left to take her to school, I started the laundry – light clothes in one tub, darks in another. My husband came back and helped me finish up. We left the house arm in arm to go to the restaurant where we both work.

9:00 – I changed into my work uniform, a red sports outfit. My first job was to clean the glass surfaces in the lobby, then the tables and chairs. We made two pots of tea to be ready for the customers and then had our breakfast. We started getting ready for the first customers, laying out tablecloths and setting the tables. It was getting cooler, so we expected business would be slow.

11:00 – We stood at the door to greet customers. (We are expected to smile and say "Welcome.") Our first customers came at about 11:30 a.m., a man and a woman. When I went to serve them tea, I noticed the man looked like he hadn't had much sleep. The woman looked tired too, even through her make-up. She may have been an evening working girl. Night life in Shanghai can be very colorful. The man ordered crab with salted egg yolk, garlic lettuce, soup, and two bowls of rice. After a while, he asked for a calculator. Now I'm in trouble, I thought. We had already started preparing the crab. What if he had changed his mind? If a customer returns an order, we have to pay for it. But it turned out that he was just figuring out the prices of the other dishes. Later, when he looked at the check, he said it seemed too high, but after going over it carefully, he was satisfied. (This is a typical Shanghai man in my mind – shrewd and tight with his money.) We were quite busy by then. The boss was glad and so were we. We worked nonstop until 3 p.m., when a co-worker went next door to bring back the lottery results. When I saw them, I realized I had won 5 yuan. Bingo! Our chef had bought quite a few tickets, but hadn't been lucky. People like us don't have much entertainment, so playing the lotto is a source of excitement. Everyone hopes to win, even if the chances are low.

16:00 – I got off work early today as a favor from my boss. After I got home, I went to buy groceries at the nearby market, as I do every day. It was bird-flu season, so I wasn't sure what to buy. I decided on celery, bean noodles, cauliflower, beans, and fish. At home, I washed the vegetables and ate a couple of crackers. Taking two more for Baobao, I rushed off to pick her up. (Most native Shanghai children are taken care of by their grandparents, but we take care of our child ourselves.) When we got home, I washed a big apple for Baobao and started making dinner. Baobao watched TV for a while and ate her apple. She likes cartoons like "Dora the Explorer."

18:30 – Baobao and I had dinner with my niece. My husband doesn't eat with us because he doesn't get home until 10 p.m. I saw how well the two girls were eating and felt good. After dinner I started reading to Baobao and taught her one or two new Chinese characters. Then we watched the educational channel.

20:30 – Baobao started getting ready for bed. She was so cute brushing her teeth, up and down, left and right. She then washed herself, including her feet, and put on fresh underwear. Her feet were like turnips, white and delicate. She had a glass of milk around 8:45 p.m. and then I tucked her in. Baobao can't seem to fall asleep unless I'm near her, so I finished my housework quickly and lay down next to her. She fell asleep right after that. I watched TV while I waited for my husband. When he came in at 10 p.m., I was relieved.

A CHAT WITH WANG XI

How long have you been living in this apartment?
More than three years. It's small for us, but we didn't want to leave our daughter with our parents back in the country, and our salaries are quite low. We share the apartment with my sister's family to save money. Shanghai is very expensive. But we feel happy living here with our child.

How old is your daughter?
She's six. People in the country all want boys, but not us. We named her Yu, which means "universe." We hope she'll go just as far as a boy.

Who cared for her when she was little?
I took care of her until three years ago, when I went back to work. Now I work part-time since I want to be there when she gets home from school.

Where does she go to school?
Her school is here in the neighborhood. It's not very expensive, about 300 yuan a month. That's still a lot of money for us, but it's worth it to stay together as a family. I want her to go all the way through school in Shanghai. But who knows …

Will that be a problem?
Primary and middle school should be fine. We'll have to pay extra to get  her enrolled, and we'll need some connections to get her into a good school. We'll also have to pay 400 or 500 yuan more than Shanghai locals per term. We'll work hard to send her to the best school, but the current policy is that she must go back to our hometown for high school unless we pay 40,000 yuan or more in fees. There's no way we could afford that.

What does she like to do?
She loves to draw. She takes drawing lessons on Sundays and gets up

early every day to draw by herself. She wants to be an art teacher when she grows up. She can also write many characters. I usually teach her a couple of new characters every day after dinner. She's also learning English.

How does she like her school?
She loves it, and her teachers seem to think very highly of her. She always wants to be their helper and do things like picking up and arranging the books.

How does one manage to bring up a helpful child like that?
I've learned a lot from the educational channel on TV. We're trying to make her independent and self-reliant. She already washes her own socks and handkerchiefs. And she listens well – I never have to repeat things to her. On the educational channel, they also talk about how to keep children from learning bad things on the Internet. She is still young and doesn't have a computer, but I already know what to do about that. We really hope that she will have a good future. It's our own future we don't quite know about.

Are you worried about that?
Our biggest worry is that she will have to go back to the country for high school. If she has to, I'll go with her, and my husband will stay here to earn money. We've already bought a little place out there just in case. We would want her to go to the best school in the area, but even that will not compare to schools in Shanghai. And university is another problem. If you graduate from a Shanghai university, it's easier to find a job than if you graduate from somewhere else.

What about your own future in Shanghai?
Because my husband is a cook, we've always wanted to open our own

restaurant. But you need the right opportunity. We actually opened a restaurant in 1999, but after three good years, our partner, who was also the owner, decided to take over the place for himself.

Did you make some money back then?

Yes, but there's only a little bit left. My husband liked to gamble at the time, and we lost almost all we'd earned. I believe we can make a good living even if we don't open a restaurant. We just have to work hard, and in a restaurant. We can't even think about having a white-collar job. I had wanted to learn how to use a computer until I heard we would only learn the basics in the course. My younger sister had done that and ended up having to go back home because she couldn't find a job here. So I gave up on the idea and devoted my time to my child.

Do you send money back to your parents?

Yes, we send money to both families, about 100 yuan every month to each. When my mother is in the hospital, we have to send at least 1,000. This year alone we've given my mother 3,000 yuan to cover her hospital bills. They don't have the kind of medical insurance or pensions in the country like they do here. Fortunately, my in-laws are in better health.

What do you think of life in Shanghai?

We've gotten used to it, but we feel like outsiders. If our child can do well here, then we'll do our best to stay.

What are your dreams and goals?

I want my daughter to have a great job and be happy. That is it. I am devoted to her future.

What do you think about China's present and future?

That's a difficult question! China has changed so fast. But migrant workers like us who do unskilled work get kind of left behind. And we're not paid like Shanghai natives. Their minimum wage is 700 yuan a month, and if they work more than eight hours, they get overtime. Employers don't have to pay migrant workers as much. And full time for us is 9 a.m. to 9 p.m., or from 4 p.m. until 4 a.m.

What do you think of Shanghai people?

Well, the men here seem to be very tight with their money. They always check the order and the bill over and over again. Our neighbors are mostly from Shanghai, but we rarely talk to them. Our work and rest times are just different. We greet each other, and that's about it. Of course, my daughter loves to say hello to her "auntie" next door. She is such a sweet talker – everyone likes her.

What are the top three things that should be changed in China?

The first thing to be changed is the unfair treatment between urban residents and people from rural areas. We came from the countryside and we feel that rural people should get the same benefits, such as pensions and insurance, because all of us are Chinese citizens. Second, the unfair  treatment towards the schooling of rural children should be changed. In my opinion, anyone who has ever left the countryside for the city is concerned with the schooling of their children, and the schooling problem is their biggest concern. The children of migrant workers should enjoy the same treatment as the children in urban areas, and they should pay the same amount of tuition. The third thing is more affordable housing. I hope to buy my own house in Shanghai. Our idea is that we sell the house in the country. By using the 200,000 yuan from selling our house in the country and our savings, we would like to buy a small apartment. Nowadays in Shanghai, a 40 m^2 apartment will cost 300,000 yuan. We are not willing to use bank loans for fear of the heavy psychological burden.

THE CONSTRUCTION WORKER'S TALE
by Xie Zheng-Yi

Shoehorned into our tiny room are two sets of bunk beds. For the privilege of living here, we four pay 150 yuan each a month. We get up every day at 5 a.m. and go off to work at different sites in the city. Today at 5 a.m., Shanghai is already stinking hot. Legs follow arms as I drag myself out from my bunk. I know that on this same morning in my hometown, the air is as cool as cool can be, and there is a slight breeze. Here in Shanghai at 6 a.m., I step outside into a filthy sauna.

We live in the northeast, and my job is on the other side of the city these days. I can't afford to take the subway, so I take the bus. It is slow and always packed. Every morning I hope to get a seat so I can close my eyes for a while. We stop and start, rocking back and forth, side to side. I have to stand the whole hour of the ride today, swaying with the bus. They lengthened our work day some time ago, and since then, I feel like I'm never quite awake, like an observer of my life.

I arrive at the public housing block I've been assigned to. Between the bus stop and the site is a spring-onion pancake stall, where I get my breakfast. I buy two pancakes. Eggs I can't afford. My job is painting the outside of the building and doing some work on the roof. When the foreman offered me the job, you'd have thought from his face that I'd just won the sweepstakes. And, in a way, I had. Painting the outside of a building is one of the easier jobs. But it was no stroke of luck for me. I'm afraid of heights, and my part of the building to paint was at the top.

The residents seem to actually hate us, maybe because we start so early. We do our best to be quiet, but some noise can't be helped. Their scowls have made us resentful. We're there to make their building more attractive, yet you would think we were there just to annoy them. Today, trudging up the stairs, I am nearly knocked over by a man rushing down. More scowls.

On the third floor, I crawl out of the window at the landing, and, keeping my eyes from the ground below, I ease myself out onto the scaffold. My slowness irritates the others. I hear their grumbling as they pass me and feel their exasperated looks. I just can't seem to move faster today. I'm so tired. I finally reach my section. I take a deep breath, open the paint bucket, and begin.

The day gets hotter and steamier, more like a Turkish bath now than a sauna. The last bite of the spring-onion pancake seems to have gotten stuck in my throat, unwilling to go down. Dripping with sweat, I climb back in through the landing window and dare to knock on a door on the third floor. A middle-aged woman opens the door. I start to ask her for a glass of water, but after a quick look at me, she closes the door in my face. I crawl back out onto the scaffold. I feel like a beaten man. I might have gotten angry in the past being treated like that, but today I feel only a certain sadness. I am so, so tired.

I don't stop for lunch, but keep working. I feel that's all I'm fit for. As I paint near a bathroom on the sixth floor, I see a young girl walk in. I don't know what I think I'm doing, but I suddenly start tapping on the window. She is startled and looks warily up at me. I make gestures to tell her of my need — pointing to my throat, tipping my head back with my mouth open, wiping my brow …

My antics must have made me look harmless, because eventually she comes to the window and opens it. I step back from the open window as far as the scaffold will allow. I don't want to scare her.

"Could I please have a glass of water?" I ask. She studies me for what seems a long time, then goes out of the room. A minute later, she returns with a tall glass of water. I drain the clear, cold water almost in one gulp. I hand the glass back to her, about to express my thanks, when she closes the window with a bang and closes the curtains. I am taken aback but not offended. Maybe she was just embarrassed. Her one small act of kindness keeps me going throughout the rest of the day.

At quitting time, the foreman shows up with our wages, which are ten days overdue. We each get 980 yuan for last month's work. He still owes us for five days, but we're so relieved about the other pay that no one says a word. We also don't want to make him mad because we might be able to get some work on the side here. Old Wu found out that many residents have been complaining about the bad condition of the windows on the inside and the clothes line frames too. We're only being paid to paint the outside, but seeing the opportunity, we have been offering to do the other work privately for 40 yuan per apartment. If we get only half the apartments to agree, that will still be over 100 yuan for each of us – that is, for Old Wu, Young Li, and me. Young Li is the best looking and also tends to have the cleanest shirt, so he's the one who has been making the initial approach to the residents. So far he's been pretty successful. If all goes according to plan, we will earn a tidy sum towards our next month's rent.

But for now I have last month's wages in my shirt pocket. My mind wanders to the pinkish light and slender hands of the girls I see through the window of a nearby hair salon. Friends of mine who came with me to the city have told me that the girls in these places will "take care of you" for 150 yuan. I sigh and think that it has been six whole months since I've seen my wife. As I walk in the direction of the pink salon, I ask myself whether one such visit is worth three to four day's work. I think of my wife waiting hopefully for the day she and our daughter can join me here. I must save so I can rent a place for us and pay for school for our child. If she can go to school here in Shanghai, perhaps she will turn out to be like that young girl today who kindly brought me water. I walk past the salon and stop at a café for dinner. I pay 5 yuan for a bowl of stir-fried rice with beef. I make the delicious food disappear, one mouthful after another, along with each of my wayward thoughts.

Xie Zheng-Yi, who holds a Bachelor of Arts in Chinese from Fudan University, is a journalist. He has published a selection of essays and was also the host of the classical Chinese "Spicy Hot Chat Room" on the Evening News.

Age 14 · **Occupation** Middle school student, outskirts of Shanghai · **Family** Mother, brother, grandparents · **Home** House in a rural area in the outskirts of Shanghai · **Free time** Taking extra classes, listening to pop music · **Monthly income (RMB)** Personal – 0; Household – 700 · **Household budget (RMB)**

CHU JUFENG

Middle school student
Outskirts of Shanghai

Housing/Utilities – 200; Education – receives scholarship to cover school fees;
Parent support – n/a; Health care – n/a; Food/Clothing/Other – 500;
Savings – n/a

"可路路，可路路" 闹钟响了，我又懒得起床了，正继在床上把我打了3个呵欠，伸了个懒腰，心想：又要开始一天的学习生活了。做好一切准备后，我却上书包，骑上自行车上学去了。因为我年龄小，所以每回母亲总会把我送到水泥路上才回家，我家离学校，每年天差不多骑十五分钟的路程，如果到回下雨的话差不多要骑二十分钟左右，骑比较远。所以每天我差不多六点左右就起床了，如果我有回家作业中有背书的，我会早起十来分钟把背书的先背一遍，才能下楼去洗脸刷牙。我一般都是六点钟就出发了，由于现在正是冬天，夜长日短，所以每天我都是在黑暗下骑车出去，有天，马路上总是空荡荡的，没有一个人，起初，我总是一步回头因为我胆小，从小我就胆小，在对看到的恐怖片太多了，总是把那些吓人的片段搬到马路上，使我感到更害怕，于是我走进一个星期后，我发觉自己的胆子变大了，不害怕黑了，所以母亲每天也就不送了。到了学校后，把自行车放到学校的停车场，然后就到教室去了。可以说我是班里来起床最早的，我是我们班最早，同学都已经在座位上复习起了功课，因为我家离学校比较远。

到了学校后，如果在回家作业中有题目没弄懂的，就乘着学习不到的同学，如果有一个同学把这道题会做了，就去请教他，就在上课把这道难弄懂的时间更长一些，许的更清楚些，学小组长和班长就把作业发给上去收那么多，然后交干到回为老师是把我和另外十个左右排在管理了，这样我也很高兴因为每天要交那么多，不用去扫也了。到7点10点钟左右老师就会到教室里来上早自修，早自修一共是七十分钟，进去我们就会做早操如果碰到下雨天，那么广播里就念讲台下的班级，今天的早操不做。"那么早自修就会延长到几十分钟，早自修后，我们是以为用功读书，报有同学都会趁着同周，进着好了下节课要用的书本什么的聊聊天，玩玩，吃点东西早自修就过去了。上午我们会上四节课，就都是上课，语文、数学、外语，物理，两堂一节课，第会有七八分钟业余时间，第二节课后会有眼保健操，眼保健操之后会舒心，上午我们上课上到11点，然后我们就有排队去食堂吃午饭，回家吃饭的，学校里吃饭要排队。

吃完饭后，我们就休息一会儿，到12点为止，开始午休，直到12点50左右，开始下午的课程，一般生下午是上四节课，上完下午第二节课也会有眼保健操，每节课之间也有七八分钟业余时间，不很频繁变课，像音乐、美术、家政、体概之类的上完回课后就放学了。但这星期五上午，下午只有两节课，也会在星期五有升旗排队，我是一座是在老师身上回，老师来给你些些学校，班级里事情，有时学校会发的，比如我班主任一到我们在班级课上总会们来些我会些方面的关心什么的。

双休回我有时会问会一起来点吃回，因为有都会跟着一个距离的同学一起回家，因为她也是骑车回她家又和我家离走十方向，不算去家比她，回近，起多分钟的路程。

双休回我家里有事就是我姑回，因为我家早要一点一刻左右才到家，我们一家人都要等回回自己一起吃饭，所以我都是晚饭吃比较晚，所以我总是先点东西再去写作业，等到双休回家后，我们就先做顶吃完顶吃饭后，我才回去作业等作业后就得差不多会，把作业里好就进两睡觉，睡前，我会把习习过。我是一天一天的学习生活就是这样，很累睡睡到八点半左右就睡觉，因为我作业差不多也到不到十点半左右，上学时回过了，我都是差不多就进的，在临睡前，我会回着今天想一想，今天都学了些什么，这是我语文老师教我们的方法，她说我们在临睡前想一想，自己今天学到了些什么回的话那么就会让自己关注自己在今天回收获些什么，哪怕的再少，那怕是知识，所以我都会在临睡前想一想自己今天学到了什么。然后，安安稳稳心里想上一句话——明天又是美好的一天，这就是我的生活。

小昆山学校 八七班 杨期月

CHU JUFENG'S DIARY

5:30 – I woke up to the ringing of my alarm clock. I yawned and stretched in bed, thinking about the day that was awaiting me. (I have to get up ten minutes earlier to practice if I have a recitation due.) I went downstairs to wash my face and brush my teeth.

6:00 – It was wintertime, with long nights and short days, so I rode my bike to school in the dark. It was still dark as I parked my bike in the school lot and went inside.

6:30 – When I entered the classroom, my classmates were already in their seats, reviewing their lessons. (I probably get up earlier than anyone else in my class, but it takes me longer than most to get here.) During this time, I might ask my classmates for help on a question from the homework. If no one can help me, I leave those questions unanswered. Then the teacher will spend more time explaining the questions. After our group leader arrived, I handed in my homework and cleaned the teacher's platform. I feel rather pleased that my teacher assigned me that job and not sweeping the floor.

7:10 – The teacher walked into the classroom for morning study hall, which lasts 40 minutes. After that we usually go out for morning exercises for ten minutes. It was raining, so we took our break inside.

8:00 – Our first class period began. We have four morning classes, usually in major subjects like Chinese, Mathematics, English, and Physics. We have a ten-minute break between each one. After the second period, we were led in exercises to maintain good eyesight and then had some cookies.

11:30 – Morning classes were over. We lined up to go to lunch in separate lines, one for those who eat at home, and the other for those who eat at school. Those of us who stay have a short rest period after lunch.

12:10 – Study hall began as usual.

13:00 – In the afternoon, we have minor subjects like Music, Art, Computers, and Physical Education. The school day ends after these four periods, but today was Friday, so we only had two periods. Instead, we had our regular class meeting, which was led by the teacher in charge of our class.

16:30 – After school, I went to buy something to eat with a friend, and we rode home together on our bikes. She goes in the same direction I do.

17:00 – Before I started my homework, I looked around for something more to eat. We don't have dinner until 6:15 p.m. or so, when my brother gets back from work. After dinner, I finished my homework and did some reading for school.

20:30 – I put my school things away and started getting ready for bed. I washed my feet, as I always do, and got into bed. Before falling asleep, I went over what I learned today, as our Chinese teacher has taught us to do at the end of the day. Then I thought to myself, tomorrow is going to be another beautiful day in my life.

A CHAT WITH CHU JUFENG

What grade are you in?
I'm in the second year of middle school, the eighth grade. My school is in Xiao Kunshan, three miles from here. My grandmother used to take me when I was younger, but I've been riding my bike to school since the fourth grade. It takes about 20 minutes.

What level of education does your mother want you to attain?
She tells me to study hard now. Of course, I have to work hard. Otherwise, I can't expect to have a happy life later. I will be in the third year of middle school next year, with just one year before the high school entrance exam. My mom wants me to go as far as possible. I enjoy studying English and I do well in English.

How old is your brother?
He's 21. He started working in a porcelain factory in Songjiang last year. He studied Mechanics and Control Systems at a technical school. His monthly salary is 700 yuan, some of which he gives us to live on. He also has a motorcycle, which costs him 100 yuan per month. His life is much better now. He's independent and has money.

What does your mother do for a living?
She's a plumber in a privately owned factory. Sometimes she has work, and sometimes she doesn't. Her average pay is a little over 500 yuan per month. And she works eight to ten hours a day.

So your mother's income, plus some help from your brother, is all your family has to live on?
Yes, the whole family, including grandparents, four people in all.

When did your father pass away?
Eight years ago. We had to depend a lot on other people's help then.

When my brother was still in school, we needed at least 300 yuan a month to live on and 4,000 yuan for school fees. We borrowed some, and the school told my mother she didn't have to pay certain things. It was a frugal life. My expenses for school now are covered by a charity – 5,000 yuan in all for two semesters, including food, tuition, school uniform, and books.

I saw your posters of singers. Whose songs do you like?
My brother likes Zhou Jielun, but I like SHE.

I see you have lots of cats. Do you have dogs, too?
No. We had a dog a couple of years ago, but it bit the old lady next door, so we had to kill it.

Were you very sad?
Not at all, we cooked it, and we ate it. The dog wasn't really a pet. It was more of a watchdog.

Are there any stories you like very much, like folk tales?
I don't care much for stories. We don't read them in school, so I hardly know any. I watched the story about Liang Shanbo and Zhu Yingtai on TV, but I don't know any foreign stories. Our Chinese textbook has mostly non-fiction pieces and narratives, most of them written in classical style. We sometimes read contemporary prose and poetry.

What do you usually do in your spare time, besides homework?
I take extra classes. I have to take extra classes every week in a lot of subjects. In the eighth grade, we have to take two one-hour classes in school on Saturday, one in English, the other in Mathematics. These are required, but they don't cost anything extra.

Do you watch TV?

We only have a few channels here, about seven or eight. But I don't spend much time watching TV, because I need to finish my schoolwork and take extra classes. I have half a day off on weekends. After Saturday classes, I sometimes go out and have some fun with my classmates. If there's time in the evening, I may watch TV for a while.

Do you like watching movies?

I like science fiction and fantasy movies. I watched Harry Potter, but it was scary. My brother likes watching movies, too, as well as playing soccer. He is good at sports. He likes to watch movies on the computer, usually horror movies.

Are you interested in news or things like that?

I don't like to watch news, but my brother does. He watches news about national affairs. And sometimes he tells us what's going on. His education level is low, so he hasn't been able to find a good job that pays well. He tells me that high school and technical school diplomas are useless and that I have to go to university if I want to have any hope for the future. He says if I don't study hard, I won't have opportunities in the future. He missed his chance, he says.

Where do your classmates live?

They all live in town, over three miles from my home. Only a few students live out here in the country, and most of them are very poor. It's expensive to live in town, but I do have a relative there, so I can stay at her place if I have to stay late at school.

How is your health?

It's okay. I did catch a cold recently. We had to run laps around the playground in gym class to stay warm. I got really sweaty and then chilled.

How long have you lived in this house?
Over ten years now. My father built it. It cost 30,000 yuan then. My father still owed people money when he died, over a third of it. We still haven't paid off the debt completely, but we're paying it back little by little.

Who gave you this church calendar?
We bought it at church. We are Christians. I don't go to church very often, just at Christmas. My mom goes more frequently, and my grandmother goes every week.

When did you start going to church?
Quite a while ago. My grandparents are religious, but I'm not. I think it's just a lot of superstitions imported from foreign countries.

What made them turn to religion?

It was their poor health. They were told that if they had faith, they would recover. There is a church in Songjiang, very near here. A lot of people in our village are faithful Christians.

What do you think about foreign countries?
Many are very well developed. We haven't studied the geography of foreign countries in school, but we did learn a little about their early history.

What worries does your family have?
My home is far from school and there are always traffic accidents on

 the road. So my mom worries about me when I ride my bike to school. It's dark when I go to school in the morning and even darker when it's raining. But once I'm in high school, I'll live at school.

Were your family and grandparents influenced by the Cultural Revolution?

Not so much, I think. There was no problem with our background.

Age 31 · **Occupation** Clothing salesman in Shanghai · **Family** Getting married soon, living with parents · **Home** Room in parents' apartment, moving into new condominium after wedding · **Free time** Shopping with fiancée, reading newspapers, watching TV, going to movies · **Monthly income (RMB)**

GAO LIJI

Clothing salesman
Shanghai

Personal – 4,500; Household – 6,500 · **Household budget (RMB)** Housing/
Utilities – 4,500; Education – 0; Parent support – 0; Health care – n/a;
Food/Clothing/Other – 1,500; Savings – 500

Gao Liji's Diary

7:30 – I got up, washed, and brushed my teeth.

7:45 – I walked from my home to the metro station and took the train to People's Square.

8:20 – When I arrived, I took a few minutes for breakfast at a snack shop before work.

8:45 – I got on the company shuttle bus near People's Square and met a colleague, who looked sleepy and dispirited. I asked him if he hadn't slept well, and he answered in a whisper that he had come home late last night after playing mahjong with friends. His wife had been so angry that she made him sleep on the sofa. I laughed at his story and gave him the nickname "Mr. Hen-pecked."

9:15 – I arrived at work.

9:30 – The sales manager held a meeting to set quarterly sales targets for the other provinces.

10:30 – I called the manager of our distributor in Hefei and asked him for his thoughts on having a New Year's promotion there.

11:30 – I had lunch in the company canteen and then played ping-pong with colleagues.

13:00 – I reviewed a new line of T-shirts for the coming season in the company showroom. We feel we have too many clothing lines for middle-aged people and are using too much cotton. I made some suggestions, such as introducing more color and variety to increase customer appeal.

17:00 – After work, our sales manager drove me to Zhongshan Park to catch the metro. I rode to People's Square and met my fiancée. We went to the Paris Wedding Photo shop to arrange for our wedding pictures. The saleswomen showed us more than 100 sample pictures and told us that what we had put down would pay for 22 photos. Additional photos would cost 180 yuan each, or we could have ten more for 1,500. We liked the samples, but couldn't afford to have them all. After much discussion, we decided to take 15 more pictures. I felt like I'd been fleeced.

19:10 – We went to Kentucky Fried Chicken, which was very crowded. My fiancée went to look for seats, while I waited in line to buy chicken burgers, french fries, coke, and chicken wings – all her favorites.

19:40 – After we finished our meal, I reluctantly agreed to go shopping with her at the Pacific Department Store. We returned home about 9:30 p.m. and then went to bed.

A CHAT WITH GAO LIJI

When did you and your fiancée first meet?
About five or six years ago. I'm nearly 32, and she is two years

younger, so it's time to get married. According to her, the Year of the Rooster is not a favorable year for marriage, but after the Chinese New Year celebration it will be the Year of the Dog so that's when we'll get married.

Congratulations! How did you two get to know each other?
We were classmates at night school.

What preparations are you making for marriage?
Oh, there is so much to be done! Decorating, buying furniture and appliances ...

I heard that it's customary in Shanghai for the man to provide the apartment and for the woman a dowry.
True. I paid for the apartment, but we bought the furniture together. She bought all the household appliances.

What else do you have to do besides decorating and furnishing?
We've got to have wedding pictures done, choose a wedding dress, and decide on the restaurant for the dinner. After checking a number of places, we decided to have our wedding dinner at the hotel for the Shanghai Foreign Language Institute. This is very expensive – it will cost me over 100,000!

So are you happy with the hotel?
It's not luxurious or so well known, but it's the right size.

What else do you have to do beforehand?
Well, we've found a wedding company, which plays a very important

role. They arrange for your wedding car, for example, and a decorated stage. And they get a master of ceremonies for you to keep the atmosphere lively and everything running smoothly. Buying the wedding dress is also complicated. You can have it made to order or rent it. We haven't made up our mind about this yet.

Who pays for the wedding?
I pay for most of it, I guess.

Have you thought about having children later on?
Yes ... Pleasure and pain always seem to go hand in hand. I think it would be great fun to have children, but they can be really annoying when they're little, especially between ages two and six.

Did you buy your apartment outright?

No, I borrowed from the bank. It cost 680,000 yuan, and I paid 210,000 down, so I have a huge mortgage. The monthly payment is a little less than 4,000. We're planning to sell our old apartment, which should be worth 500,000 or 600,000. With some additional help from my parents, I should be able to pay off the mortgage relatively fast.

How's your work?
I work as a salesman for a clothing company. I've been there for four years and before that, I was also in sales at another company. I started working in 1995 when I was 21 or so.

You have a lot of experience then. How's the job going?
Not bad. Monthly salary plus bonus, that comes to a bit more than 4,000 yuan, and sometimes it's even more than that. That's enough to cover our monthly mortgage payment.

How's your company doing?

Competition is intense, and we've got large inventories. But my boss believes in the Chinese market and is investing heavily in it. Our inventories are high because of the wide range of styles we offer and the increasing selectivity of customers. So we have to work hard to find new outlets for our products. When sales in Shanghai are not good, we try to shift to other locations.

How do you determine whether your products will sell outside of Shanghai?

First, we research the local market. When we arrive at a city for the first time, we buy a map and start asking people where the busiest streets are. We walk around there and estimate customer volume. We consider things like the availability of major brands, the level of customer satisfaction, and people's purchasing power. We also talk to shopping mall managers about promotional activities and things like that. Another approach is to look for new dealers, but that takes time. Franchising is another possibility. I'm on the road a lot, more than two weeks a month on average. Luckily, my fiancée doesn't complain much about it.

What are your plans for the future?

I don't have other skills, just sales. If I work another five or ten years for my company, I should be able to move up, but they may ask me to relocate to another province. If I stay in Shanghai, I might start my own business one day.

Have you ever thought about buying a car?

Yes, but not now. Eventually I want to buy an affordable car, like a Polo. But right now my biggest concern is paying down my mortgage in the shortest time possible. I should have no big pressure after that, and life should be much better.

What are your other major concerns right now?

Just the mortgage. My parents are in good health, so I don't have much else to worry about, but this could become a concern soon. My life is not bad, and my job is good.

After you get married, will your cost of living rise?

Probably. My fiancée earns a bit more than 2,000 yuan a month, and  I bring in a little over 4,000. But we actually consume very little and only buy things we really need. Apart from savings, we spend the rest of our money on entertainment, clothing, and utilities. We don't spend a lot on food.

Do you watch or read about national news?

I don't have much interest in that. It's really not my concern. I know who our national leaders are, of course. If I didn't, people would think I was from Mars.

Are you a member of the Youth League or the Communist Party?

I joined the Youth League in middle school. As for the Communist Party, my firm doesn't encourage people to join. If you do, the boss is likely to complain that you're using his time for the Party.

What do you think about the world outside of China?

I never pay any particular attention to other countries — though I think America is always meddling in others' affairs; Japan is double-dealing; South Korea is feudal; Australians are peasants; and Canada doesn't matter. From television, I have gotten a favorable impression of Europe, though, because of its long history, social welfare system, and environment.

THE STUDENT'S TALE

by Jiang Fang-Zhou

At 6 a.m. I get up. Well, that's not strictly true. Before I get up, I spend some time mulling over my dreams. But I'm not going to tell you about my dreams, because they happen before 6 a.m.

Before I leave the dorm, I always put on my bracelet. It's very cool. It's genuine leather and has "KILL" burned into it. Not that I'm superstitious, but I am convinced that it wards off all kinds of bad luck. Right now, bad luck includes the otherwise sought after Plum Blossom Luck (falling in love). Falling in love, for me, would only be a distraction.

I don't want to even think about guys while I'm still in school. Everyone agrees that it can only wreck your grades. And I can't let that happen. The admission exam to get into this place — a very select senior high school, I can tell you — I found hard enough to pass. So I know that I'm going to have to work even harder to get into a first-rate university. Like all students, I hear the same refrain practically every day from my parents: "You won't amount to a hill of beans if you don't go to college! Do you want to end up driving a three-wheeled cart for a living?" But we're all used to it by now. We've been hearing it since we were born.

Ten minutes after I have left the dorm, you will find me near the jogger throng on the school sports field. I'm not likely to be jogging, though. Walking is more my style, except when we're dismissed. Then no one runs faster to the school canteen than I do. For breakfast I have two meat-filled dumplings. No soft drinks, no porridge. That would take too much time. I only allow myself five minutes for breakfast, which means I basically don't look up from my food. One morning, one of the most gorgeous guys in my class sat down right across from me and I didn't pay him any attention. Mind you, like most senior high school students, I am terribly near-sighted. A senior high school student who is not near-sighted is a rare bird in China today.

The first period starts at 7 a.m. sharp. The three most important subjects for me, the ones that are the backbone of the college entrance exam, are Literature, Math, and English. In these three, I absolutely have to perform. It helps that our teacher for Chinese Literature is a tall, attractive woman, and our Math teacher helps the lesson along by making jokes. Still, the subjects are so mind-numbingly dull. How anyone can get excited about ancient Chinese Literature or trigonometry is beyond me.

During the day, I have nine classes, and in the evening, I have three study halls. This means that I spend twelve hours in the classroom five days a week. And if you think that's over the top, let me tell you that I am envied by those still in junior high. They have to spend even more time in the classroom — and on weekends too. All they get is half a day off per week! Why do they do it? Quiet now ... listen carefully, and I think you'll hear their parents over there also saying, "Do you want to end up driving a three-wheeled cart for a living?"

As I said, this is a very select school. Some of the courses here are not available in other, less select schools. Today, for instance, we have English Conversation. This is taught by Julian, who is a very handsome young man from Australia. Today he brought in some soap, toothpaste, and shower gel and he had us make up advertising slogans for them. My team won a bar of soap from the school convenience store. Lesson over, Julian took the bar of soap with him — to reward the next team, we could only presume. We get Julian only once a week. All of our other English lessons are given by Chinese teachers.

Today I also had IT. The school has an IT room with 60 computers, so each of us has access. We also have two physical education classes every week. I usually play ping-pong or badminton. Then, after 4 p.m., we have various options. We can take jazz dancing, martial arts, guitar, basketball, extra biology, and so on. My parents persuaded me to put my name down for extra math. And it's perfectly true: I don't want to end up driving a three-wheeled cart.

Between classes, I chat with my friends. I don't like talking to guys, probably because I don't know what to say to them. With the other girls, I talk about pop stars mostly. And the pop stars are mostly from America, Korea, and Taiwan. Or, if someone's noticed a guy giving a girl the eye, then we'll talk about that, of course. That will get talked about so much it will be all over the school in no time. Last week I heard that this guy had such a crush on this girl that he asked a friend of hers to get him a pair of her panties. Yuck!

Between classes, I quickly check my mobile for any messages. Officially, we're not supposed to have mobiles in school. But every student here does, as far as I can see, even those who don't have a lot of money.

I eat breakfast, lunch, and dinner in the school canteen. We have a choice of three meals. They cost 3, 4, or 5 yuan. To keep to my 10 yuan a day budget, I usually have the 3-yuan meal. I confess, though, I spend a small fortune on snacks and fruit, and I always treat myself to some milk.

On Sunday my parents visit and take me shopping, usually for clothes. This has become a largely pointless exercise, however. What pleases them displeases me. Or, put another way, their taste is most definitely uncool. The consequence: We come home empty-handed every time.

When I'm not spending time with my parents on Sunday, I usually go to the underground music market to see what I can pick up in the way of European and American CDs. My taste leans towards Christina Aguilera, Shakira, and Elton John.

Also – and I have to tell you that I really, really do not want to drive a three-wheeled cart – I go out and buy books filled with mock exams. You can get these in most bookshops. And every day, on my own time,

I will slog through 10 to 20 pages of the stuff. As I've been told at least once, I have to get into one of the better universities if I want to amount to at least a hill of beans. In all seriousness, since the day I was born, my parents have been putting money aside for my education. I don't want to let them down.

Call me superstitious if you like, but I get into bed at precisely 22:22:22 every night. I don't think the people who run this senior high school are necessarily superstitious, but they turn out the lights every night just as precisely, at 22:30:00. Very soon, however, one becomes aware of small yellow glimmerings in the room. These yellow glimmerings emanate from students in their final year. By flashlight they are working through mock exam after mock exam. This leads me to conclude there will be very few three-wheeled cart drivers graduating from our school this year.

Jiang Fang-Zhou is a senior high school student. She has already published seven books in China.

Age 26· Occupation "Mamasang" (senior hostess/manager) at a KTV (karaoke) bar in Shanghai · **Family** Single · **Home** 60 m², three-bedroom apartment, plus own house in hometown in Hubei province · **Free time** Shopping · **Monthly income (RMB)** Personal – 60,000; Household – 60,000

Ms. Wang

KTV hostess
Shanghai

Household budget (RMB) Housing/Utilities – 4,000; Education – n/a; Parent support – 10,000; Health care – 500; Food/Clothing/Other – 5,500; Savings – 40,000

Ms. Wang's Diary

20:00 – My workday at the KTV bar began. I greeted my first customers – a Chinese and a Korean businessman. I showed them ten girls in their room salon. They picked two, Wen-wen and Lu-lu. This room is equipped with very good karaoke equipment for the girls and customers to play around with. The customers sang terribly, so we laughed a lot. I ordered some delicious food and drinks for everyone, which of course the customers pay for.

20:15 – I left that room because many of my other customers are waiting. (On average I "greet" for about seven rooms and over the weekend I sometimes have more than ten rooms to cover).

22:30 – The Korean businessman in the first room was complaining because Lu-lu had to occasionally sneak out to entertain another regular customer of hers. Lu-lu is a "well-built" girl and many men like her. And very often she has to juggle customers between two rooms. So I found the Korean guy another similar-looking girl and he seemed to be ok for now.

24:00 – I had an argument with one of my customers after he did not tip the waitress enough. He didn't think she was attentive enough, so didn't want to pay. I got his colleague to pay. I am responsible for making sure we collect the money.

2:00 – The end of my workday, about six hours in all. They started closing up the bar as I went outside and found a taxi to take me home. I fell asleep almost immediately once I got home.

12:00 – I got up to get something to eat – some leftovers from the night before, then went back to bed for a while. I woke up remembering I wanted to send my parents money and also go shopping for some clothes and make-up. I try to send my parents 10,000 yuan a month because they both have health problems. They really need the money, but I can only send that much when business is good because I am trying to save as much as possible so that one day I can start my own business. Fortunately, my older sister also works and can help them, too, though my little brother can't because he's still in high school.

16:00 – I left my apartment to take care of my errands. Just as I was leaving I ran into my maid, who comes for two hours every day to clean and cook for me.

18:30 – I came home and ate the dinner she left for me. Afterwards, I took a shower, got into my nice clothes, and left to go to work.

A CHAT WITH MS. WANG

How long have you been working in this business?
Many years. I came here when I was 15 from Hubei province in 1995.

I understand you're in a high position for someone your age.
That's true, I guess. I used to work at another KTV, but my boss lured me away five years ago. I have been able to bring in a large number of guests, so I've been promoted, step by step, to my present position.

How do you get promoted in this business?
You have to have a certain number of regular customers. That's part of what they look at. But you also have to have volume. You have to bring in around 100,000 yuan a month in revenues for the owner. Once you get promoted, you still have to take care of your customers, but you don't have to entertain them in the room salons. A typical manager earns 300 yuan per room and can fill many rooms in an evening. A nightclub operator has any number of managers, or mamasangs, to help him run the business. It's their job to train and supervise the hostesses and waitresses. The hostesses entertain the guests, of course, and the waitresses serve refreshments, do general cleaning, and keep track of who is in what private room when. Most mamasangs are former hostesses who demonstrated an ability to generate a high volume of business. Waitresses are generally of  a different type – they're younger and maybe not as pretty. Most of them don't become hostesses later, but they can earn tips of up to 200 yuan per room per night. Sometimes they get more tips than the hostesses because some guests just prefer them. But guests aren't allowed to do more than a little hugging on the dancefloor with them.

How do you find new hostesses?
We hire them from all over, frequently from outside of Shanghai, usually

from small cities and rural areas. For example, Lu-lu, the girl you just met, came to Shanghai from Dalian two years ago after she graduated from a technical high school. She used to sell computers in Metro City,  but she didn't get along with her boss, so she was eventually fired. So her friend, who is also working here, arranged an introduction. Look, this is her working card issued by the government. There's a number on it, just like on our ID. We have quite a few high school graduates, even university students. We used to have a couple of models here, too, but not anymore. They went to one of the new KTVs that opened a while ago. It's big and luxurious. The hostesses there wear traditional Chinese dress and earn a lot of money.

How do they like their job here?
It's okay. Business is quite good. We have lots of competition though. There are so many KTVs in Shanghai. But it's still quick money.

How much does it cost to open a KTV bar like this in Shanghai?
About 30 million yuan, I would say. But I wouldn't advise anyone to go into the nightclub business now. There are too many of them in Shanghai already. And running this kind of business is by no means easy. A number of bars here have had to close down recently. Of course we are doing alright. We have 148 room salons. The average fee per room is 1,000. Drinks can be expensive – one bottle of XO will cost you 2,500. The owner makes about 30 million a year.

How much can a hostess earn in a month?
It ranges between 7,000 and 10,000 yuan a month, all in tips. They get 300 yuan from each customer. Take Lu-lu as example, when she sold computers, she was earning about half of that and had to work much longer hours, basically from ten in the morning until ten at night.

This is much easier. Lu-lu is even thinking about moving to Singapore next year. She's got some friends there and they can get her some introductions.

Can you tell me what your typical customer is like?

 We get all kinds – mainly Chinese (government employees, businessmen, tourists). There are also many foreigners, from Taiwan, Hong Kong, Japan, Korea, and other countries. That's why some of us speak English or Japanese. We get a lot of men who are in Shanghai on business, or for conferences. Their local colleagues bring them. There are also some regulars from around here. Some come almost every day, maybe 20 times a month.

How many customers come into your KTV on an average night?

Well, tonight, business is better than expected. We don't have enough girls to take care of all the customers. They can each take at most two customers a night. But business overall, as I said, is slower these days. There are about 200 hostesses and 70 mamasangs now, but in the past, there were more than 1,000 hostesses and 400 mamasangs.

How do the hostesses usually entertain their customers?

Well, you know that their customers come here not because they want to sing – they could go to a much cheaper place to sing Karaoke. The customers come here because of these girls. They spend a lot of time talking – they usually talk about their personal matters, their frustrations, sex, friends. Some customers like it when the girls touch them – they will of course try and fondle the girls. The only girl they cannot fondle is the waitress.

Are your customers generally well-behaved?

Of course, like everywhere, there are good people and bad people.

But they all seem to like a sexy looking girl. Some customers will want to have sex and will pay more than 2,000 yuan for that. They usually will take the girls to their hotels or even their apartments. Of course, that's the girls' own choice.

Do your customers tend to be married, or single?
We never ask about things like that. But most are relatively well-off middle-aged men, and many are wearing a wedding ring. I guess I would say there are more married men than single men. But some ask the hostesses out and even want to take them home.

Do you teach your hostesses about safe sex?
They are not encouraged to provide sexual services to guests, but they are adults and know what precautions are advisable. We have had no problems in that regard, no cases of AIDS or anything like that.

Do you have a boyfriend?
I have many boyfriends. I haven't thought about marriage yet, and I won't until I get out of this line of work. A former boyfriend of mine lives in the U.S. I would like to go there and maybe visit him, but my application for a commercial visa was rejected.

What would you like to do once you get out of this work?
I don't know yet. I have many ideas. One thing I know is that I want to stay here in Shanghai and not go back to the provinces. I also want to learn Japanese, since I have many Japanese guests. But for the longer term, maybe running a restaurant would be fun, though you can't make much money with a small one, and a big one requires a lot of money. What I really need to do  is find a business partner, but all the people with money seem to be men, and I don't want to work with a male partner. Some friends of

mine are raising crocodiles and selling health care products in Jiangsu, and they asked me whether I wanted to invest. I have visited them, but haven't made any decision as yet.

Are you able to save a reasonable amount of money?
Yes. I bought a house in Wuhan, which I have in addition to the apartment I rent near here. I was also able to buy this diamond in Hong Kong. I am also very determined to keep depositing money in the bank. And I'm very determined to be my own boss. I don't think I can just help somebody do their work. I met a man in Hong Kong a while back and he keeps calling me to join his company as a secretary, working from eight to five, which would be a real job. But even with a bonus of several thousand yuan, I wouldn't be earning much money. Here, I can make 50,000 or 60,000 yuan in a month. What would you do?

Age 50 · **Occupation** Night watchman in a music CD and cassette factory in Shanghai · **Family** Wife, 21-year-old daughter · **Home** 70 m², two-bedroom apartment · **Free time** Watching TV, shopping with wife, reading newspapers, meeting old classmates in teahouses · **Monthly income (RMB)** Personal –

FAN YOUYI

Night watchman
Shanghai

2,500+; Household – 4,000+ · **Household budget (RMB)** Housing/Utilities
300; Education – 2,500; Parent support – 0; Health care – 200; Food/
Clothing/Other – 1,000; Savings – n/a

12月28日

　　早上7点钟起床，梳洗之后，7点15分与找钱人一起去菜场购买蔬菜等。其中买了芹菜，1元一斤，大白菜一棵八角一斤，豆芽0.5一斤买了1元。香菇菜7毛一斤买4.5元，小鲫鱼5元一斤买了1斤。8点钟回家吃早饭，吃了面包和牛奶。吃好早饭后，8点45分同找钱人一起出门。乘隧道三线到人民广场站下来，到青问路中国人寿保险公司领取女儿读书的教育基金，每年400元，和找钱人的两份养老保险金。10点15分再好出来。一路走到市百一店地方去买帮找钱人买了一双休闲鞋，牌子是佳福来。买好后时间已到11点15分了，我们就走到福建中路河南路口的德兴面馆，一人吃一碗闷蹄双鲜面，价格为7元一碗。吃好以后再走到延安东路浙江路站乘隧道三线到浦东八佰伴站下来，到家已是12点40分。东西放好，休息一下，下午同找钱人又一起出门。乘1点15分去8大自场易初莲花超市去购物。买了羊肉卷、包心菜元、包心鱼元、亲亲肠、台湾菜元、海螺元、麦风云吞、大白兔山豆奶粉，雅士利加应子等食品。再来下午3点钟飞大写场方面班回家，3点另5分到家，把东西放好，然后我爱人看电视，我就休息睡了一会，到4点3分起来准备烧晚饭，晚上炒青菜，煮了小排鱼，蹄膀红烧，香梦，杏鲍菇，西期芽，肉丝，炒丸一起，另外烧了一锅汤，放了鱼丸、贝壳、虾丝、自煲等，晚上6点吃晚饭，边吃饭边看电视，内容为新闻节目，晚上7点半去上夜班，8点钟到单位值班，到单位后，夜里看报纸，有新闻晨报、劳动报等，听广播，12点半以后休息，到第二天早上8点钟下班。

贺如贻

FAN YOUYI'S DIARY

7:00 – I didn't have to work last night. My wife and I got up, dressed, and went to the market to buy vegetables. We bought greens, Chinese cabbage, and bamboo shoots.

8:00 – Back home, we had bread and milk for breakfast.

8:45 – We left home and took the subway to People's Square. We went to China Life Insurance, where we withdrew the stipend for our daughter's education as well as my wife's pension.

10:15 – In the basement of Department Store No.1, my wife bought a pair of shoes.

11:15 – We stopped at a restaurant nearby for a bowl of pork trotter noodles. Then we took the subway a few stations and got off at the Pudong New District stop.

12:40 – After arriving home and putting our things away, we took a short nap.

13:15 – We left the apartment and caught the 1:19 pm shuttle bus to the Lotus Supermarket at Superbrand Mall. We bought mutton, meat balls, fish balls, mini-sausages, Taiwan meat balls, mini-dumplings, red bean candy, and plum preserves.

15:00 – We caught the shuttle bus and were home some five minutes later. After putting the bags down, my wife watched some TV, and I went to the bedroom for a nap.

16:40 – In the kitchen, I put some greens, fish, pork trotter, bamboo shoots, and meat balls together in a pot and let it cook slowly.

18:00 – We watched the news while we ate my stew.

19:00 – I left for the night shift.

20:00 – I began work. I usually read the newspaper there, including the Xinming Evening Newspaper, and listen to the radio. I usually sleep from 10:30 p.m. to 5 or 6 a.m. Nothing usually happens – just the odd person asking for directions. My employer allows me to do that, especially in light of the health problems I have had.

8:00 – I left work for home.

A CHAT WITH FAN YOUYI

How long have you lived here?
11 years. We used to live on Pu Dian Road in another public housing building, but that place was torn down and we were resettled here. The neighborhood is convenient and nice – we're right across the street from some very exclusive apartments – but I've heard that our building is going to be torn down. They're probably making room for some new, high-end apartments.

What kind of compensation did you get when you were resettled before?
We got an apartment instead of money back then. How much room you got depended on how many people were in the family. But the space we were allotted wasn't enough, so my work unit took up a collection for me. With that, we were able to get ourselves an extra 6 m^2.

Where do you and your wife work?
I work for an audio-visual publishing company, and my wife just retired from there. I had surgery last year, so my employer assigned me to the job of night watchman, which is a less demanding job than what I had before.

Are you working full time?
No, I work on alternating days, which means I work three days one week and four days the next. That amounts to three and a half days a week – and no weekends.

What surgery did you have?
It was terrible. I suddenly found myself unable to walk. They found that my lumbar nerves were blocked, so they operated. I've recovered fairly well from the surgery, otherwise I'd be forced to sit in orthopedic chairs

154

like this for the rest of my life. My wife is not in very good health, either. She has had two operations herself.

How do you feel about the medical care reform?
In the past, all medical expenses were covered once you met the minimum service requirement. Now you have to pay 10 percent yourself. Recent retirees, like my wife, pay 1,280 yuan for hospitalization and 770 for outpatient care. Everything is fine as long as you're well. But you face huge expenses if you get sick.

What do you think about doctors these days?
I would say that the responsible doctors still outnumber the irresponsible ones. But you have to know the rules of the game. If you don't offer a red envelope with a nice tip, you will probably be operated on by a junior surgeon with little experience. And experienced surgeons are generally just better.

What do you think of tipping doctors?

Some surgeons won't do an operation unless they get something. Others operate either way. My surgeon actually refused to take a tip, so I bought some books for his child. I felt good about doing that, and he accepted them. Doctors work very hard today and don't always earn a lot. I know an excellent surgeon who never accepts a tip. I once saw him eating a bowl of instant noodles – his dinner between patients. I felt sorry for him somehow. He was working so hard that he didn't have the time for a proper dinner, much less a decent rest between patients.

How difficult is it to finance your daughter's education?
Well, tuition is 10,000 and room and basic board 13,000 yuan per semester. Meals and other expenses for her come to nearly 2,000 yuan

per month. But she has a stipend, and we have been working at good jobs for many years. We also have some savings. We think we can manage for the time being.

What does your daughter hope to do after graduation?
She wants to get a job. She studies very hard – when she was in high school she studied every night until 11 p.m. She has a very specialized major (Electrical Engineering), so there shouldn't be a problem. Some of her classmates are considering  studying abroad, but we can't afford that, and we really don't want our daughter to go abroad. Why not just stay in China and find a good job? The cost of living is much higher abroad. You may earn more, but you have to spend more. We Shanghai people live a relatively better life (compared with other parts of China), but the situation will totally change if one goes abroad. Think of those migrant workers in Shanghai. I often think that people who go abroad are just like those migrant workers coming to Shanghai.

What is your feeling about migrant workers in Shanghai?
I don't have any definite opinions about them, and I am not hostile towards them. It's not easy for them to leave their families. There are also very good people among them. They study hard and put up with a lot of hardships. But sometimes they are very unlucky. Some are paid well and get other benefits if they work for a responsible company, but others get cheated by unscrupulous employers. On the whole, though, I think migrant workers are treated pretty well in Shanghai.

Do you follow national affairs?
Yes, but mostly when the issue is directly related to our life. Medical insurance – that's probably our biggest concern in that sense. We're also worried about where we're going to live after resettlement. But

other than that, we're generally not worried. Our daughter's future is in her hands. We have provided her with everything we can.

Do you think the government is making progress fighting corruption?
It's better now. The government is disclosing more than in the past – like about all those coal miners who died in the explosion last year. We never would have heard about that. Workers like us feel that President Hu Jintao has really done something good in this respect.

What impressions do you have of foreign countries?
The U.S. is too bullying, Japan is irritating, and China is too weak. I know the U.S. is building some missile defense system that targets China. The Americans talk about protecting Taiwan, but their missile system is actually aimed at China. We learn about this from TV. To be frank, I feel that Chinese people are still not that respected abroad yet.

Age 25 · **Occupation** Engineer/Manager at a multinational company in Shanghai · **Family** Wife, newly married · **Home** 80 m², two-bedroom condominium · **Free time** Travel, photography, watching TV · **Monthly income**

CHEN LIANG

Engineer at an MNC
Shanghai

(RMB) Personal – 10,000; Household – 15,000 · **Household budget (RMB)**
Housing/Utilities – 4,500; Education – 0; Parent support – n/a; Food/
Clothing/Other – 2,500+; Savings – 8,000

Chen Liang's Diary

6:50 – It's a struggle to get out of bed every morning, especially in winter. But if we're late getting up, by even just a few minutes, we would miss the bus.

7:20 – We catch the shuttle bus in front of our building. My wife booked this for us – a Ford minibus – through a network of drivers who take passengers with destinations along their route. The driver is a funny middle-aged man, who drives to work with his wife and daughter every day. He drops us off at the Lu Jiazui station, where we take the subway. My wife's plan is really very good. My company is 16 kilometers from my home. All in all, it takes about an hour to get there.

8:30 – Not many people are at work when I arrive, but the boss and the team leader are always there before me. I wash my hands, then sit down and check my e-mails. We typically exchange ideas with our U.S. headquarters via e-mail, but some things have to be discussed on the phone, and on those days, I have to be at work earlier. In design, where I work, our daily set of tasks is seemingly endless. In the two and a half years since I started here as an inexperienced graduate, I have nonetheless learned to be self-reliant.

12:00 – I go to lunch at the company canteen. There are usually five dishes to choose from, but I'm tired of them by now because they're pretty much the same every day. After lunch, I often play ping-pong with my colleagues in the entertainment room or take care of personal business.

13:20 – Back at my desk, I already feel behind schedule. There is so much to do, even though there are more work hours in the afternoon than in the morning. But I become immersed in my work and forget everything else.

18:00 – If I don't have to work overtime for some reason, I usually call my mother to tell her I'll go to her place for dinner. My wife and I meet at the Lu Jiazui station and take a bus or taxi from there. Because overtime is becoming a way of life at our company, we usually manage to eat together only once a week.

21:00 – This is when I come home if I have to work late. The company pays for a taxi at least, which helps. When I get home, I talk briefly with my wife, then take a bath and lie down with my wife to watch TV. We have satellite TV, so we can watch BBC, CNN, and movies. This is the happiest part of my day.

24:00 – Time to sleep.

A CHAT WITH CHEN LIANG

I hear your wedding is coming up soon – congratulations!
Thank you. Actually, we were officially married over a year ago, but then my father passed away, so we waited a year to celebrate.

What happened to your father?
He died of liver cancer. He was only 53. He suffered a lot last year and was in the hospital most of it. He had had hepatitis ten years earlier, but had taken fairly good care of himself afterwards. Later, he began having severe pain. My father was operated on by the best surgeon in the field, but the surgeon was unable to completely remove the tumor. The only hope was that he might recover through rest and a healthy diet. The care from the hospital was very poor.

They couldn't perform another operation?
No. His liver function was very weak, and the incision was healing poorly. He didn't tell his company he had cancer. My mother was asked many times how he was doing and had to make up all kinds of stories.

Why didn't your father tell his company?
He didn't want to cause other people trouble. Also, if he had told them, people would have come to see him in the hospital, and he wouldn't have been able to get any rest. After the operation, the hospital asked him to leave because there was no hope of a cure there. They recommended we go to a local hospital for other treatment.

If his company didn't know about this, how were his medical bills paid?
We had some savings as a family, and my mother and I also drew from our income. My father did have medical insurance, but not enough. The costs over that year ran between 90,000 and 100,000 yuan.

Did you give doctors money in red envelopes?
Yes, you give a little more to those with whom you have a good

relationship. For a typical relationship between doctor and patient, you give between 500 and 1,000 yuan. If he says he cannot accept cash, you just buy a public transport card of 500 yuan. The general sentiment in this society is that if you don't give doctors money in red envelopes, doctors will not treat your disease seriously.

Your father died relatively young – has it changed your outlook on life?
It was the toughest time of my life, but it made me stronger. After that, I don't think there's anything I can't face. When I reflect back, I don't  think I've experienced many situations where I was so dependent on others to solve my problem. But there are always problems around, like inefficiency or corruption, especially in the government. You see stories about it all the time on TV. I also have classmates who are public servants. So many are only interested in acquiring power and money. It's not that I'm completely disillusioned, but I have seen so much of this kind of thing, even in my generation.

Does this make you lose confidence in China's progress?
Many my age feel that the state has a stranglehold on our money. The cost of living is very high – water, power, and gas are terribly expensive. We also pay high taxes. The problem is, it's hard to see what they do with our tax money, and when they do something, it takes a long, long time. I pay over 20 percent in taxes and contribute 3 percent of my salary to the retirement fund. Our contributions should be put into a personal account, but the government manages it instead all together in an aggregate account.

What are your dreams for the future?
For the moment, I am trying desperately to make enough money to pay for a proper wedding. A wedding in Shanghai costs a lot, especially

if you want to have 30 tables, like we do. We're both from Shanghai, so there are many relatives who can come. The guests will give us money in red envelopes, but the investment must come from us. With wedding pictures, bridal gown, dinner, and other expenses, our total budget will run between 80,000 to 90,000 yuan – all our savings so far – and that doesn't even include the honeymoon.

All your savings?
Yes. After all, marriage is a once-in-a-lifetime event. It should be a very special celebration.

Have you been to other countries or other parts of China?
I studied in Singapore, and from there I visited Malaysia once. I also have been to Russia on vacation. I love traveling and taking pictures. I go somewhere at least once a year. During Christmas, I took my wife to Qingdao for a holiday. This year my company will send me to our U.S. headquarters for a month.

What are your impressions of other foreign countries?
All I know about them is what I see on TV or read on the Internet. I understand the quality of education in the U.S. is very high.

What has been your career path so far?
When I graduated from university, I took a job writing software for a Japanese company, but I wasn't happy. Here, I am involved with hardware, which is more closely related to my education. To me, liking your job is the most important thing. I like what I do now, and my performance is steadily improving. I feel my boss is beginning to appreciate my work, little by little.

How do you see your career unfolding over the next five to ten years?
My hope is to gain broader experience by working in different parts of the company. I admire my boss very much and would like to become more like him. He had many years' experience working in big companies in the U.S., and came back to run the China operation three years ago. I am also optimistic about the company's chances here in China. Although I once thought of starting my own business or going into partnership with several others, having a stable income to support my family is ultimately more important. Going on your own is something more for my wife. She has the courage, energy, and desire. She also would like to be free from the constraints of working for a company. So I guess I'm the stable factor in this relationship ...

THE TALE OF THE MASSAGE GIRLS
by Xiao Yi

I – One Massage Girl

The street lamps are not working. In this suburb, they never seem to get repaired. But at 3 a.m., there's hardly anyone else around anyway. She turns the corner. She doesn't see what hits her. The last thing she sees is her bag falling and jars of cream and bottles of oil scattering across the road.

On a tree-lined avenue near the city center is the very best sauna in town. It has impressive front doors that open into a wide corridor. At 6 on the dot every evening, she passes through these doors and enters the employee changing room. There, she changes into her work clothes and then goes out to the sauna lobby and stands in front of rows and rows of beauty products. Some of these she uses for her massages. Others she recommends for clients to use at home. She is proud of her knowledge about these products and of her skill at massage. She waits.

Business doesn't begin to pick up until after dinner, usually after 9 p.m. Then men and women start coming in, sometimes together. The man may be pot-bellied, and his companion young and attractive. When the woman is older, then she is very well dressed and well coiffed, perhaps with a watchful look in her eyes. When an older woman reappears wrapped in her white Turkish towels after a bath or a sauna, she will ask for a massage from her, not from the younger, pretty massage girls.

In the massage room, she always turns her back while the woman takes off her towels and climbs onto the massage table. Then she begins to smooth onto her back one of the creams or oils she has chosen from the rows and rows of beauty products in the lobby.

The body begins to tell its story under her touch. Some are skinny, others fat. Some are well taken care of and clean, others are not. Some have one scar, one story. Some look as if they have never known pain, never known poverty. Others have stretch marks and feel tired to the touch, still others relax under her hands. None, though, is like hers. None has a story like hers. This is her fate.

Sometimes, as she gently works her fingers into their flesh, she tells them in a low, soothing monotone of her own life, how she came to the city six years ago and goes back home once a year. She talks about the other massage girl, the one she lives with in a dormitory, about how they get up at noon, have breakfast, and clean up the rooms. Sometimes, she tells them what she did that day, that she went to pay her phone bill or that she sent presents to her children.

If the client rouses herself, woman to woman, to ask of her children, she tells them that she saves all she can for them, lives on as little as she can, just enough to make herself respectable for work. And here at work she is, every single day. From 6 p.m. until 2 a.m., when she then bathes and has something to eat in the canteen before she goes home. And she tells her client that, as she leaves, she sees other massage girls in the sauna restaurant having dinner and listening to loud music. How they bear it, she cannot imagine. Isn't the noise of the streets every day enough?

At 3 a.m. she will be walking home through her suburb's poorly lit streets.

II – Another Massage Girl
The street lamps are not working. In this suburb, they never seem to get repaired. But at 3 a.m., there's hardly anyone else around anyway. She turns the corner. Her motorcycle hits something, throws her to the ground. The last thing she sees is a bag falling and jars of cream and bottles of oil scattering across the road.

The massage girl works in a small sauna nearby. It is not quite what it seems. She started to work there after she quit middle school. At first, she was a maid, fetching and carrying for the massage girls. Then, to make more money, she became a massage girl herself. Then, to make even more money, she began performing other services for her clients. Money is money is money is money, has been her philosophy. The only difference is who has it and how freely it flows.

She'd had a boyfriend then, in the beginning. But he didn't like what she was doing for her clients. "How can you have sex without feelings?" he would ask her. "What good are feelings?" she would reply, "Feelings won't pay the bills." He soon left her.

This is not the life she once dreamed of for herself. But it is the life she has, and she knows she is the only person who will get her what she wants. What she wants are beautiful clothes, expensive jewelry – a life of luxury, in short. And to get it, she only needs to use her body. So she gets up at noon, eats breakfast, does her exercises, then goes for a swim. In the late afternoon, she may go out for dinner with her boyfriend at the time, or maybe with friends. After work at the sauna, if she is not totally exhausted, she may go downtown with a client or with the other girls to have a late dinner.

Her boyfriend has a wife somewhere. He was one of those clients who took her downtown to eat after work. Now she often sees him outside of work, sometimes she even massages him for free. When he can get away, he will often book the last massage of her day. Tonight, he came on his new motorcycle and took her for a ride. When they got back, she begged him to teach her how to ride. Sitting behind her, he told her how to drive.

After a while, he said he wanted to buy some cigarettes, so they stopped. She told him that when she was rich and had her own house and swimming pool, she was going to get herself the coolest, fastest motorcycle in the world and beat every leather-clad biker on the road.

He laughed and told her that she'd better practice some more before that. So she drove off on her own while he smoked his cigarette. As the bike picked up speed, the wind almost stopped her breath, but she loved the way her hair rippled behind her, the thrum of the engine beneath her. Then she came to a corner.

As she turned the corner, she felt an impact, then was thrown off the motorcycle. The last thing she saw was a bag falling open and jars and bottles scattering across the street.

III – The police
When the police arrived, there was nothing to be seen but two women lying motionless in the street, not far from each other. No motorcycle, just broken jars and bottles sending sweet perfume into the air.

Xiao Yi's publications include two novels, "The Blue Nail" and "Desirable Eyes," and several translated works.

Age 18 · **Occupation** Migrant restaurant worker in Shanghai · **Family**
Single · **Home** 20 m² dormitory room shared with six co-workers · **Free
time** Surfing at Internet bar, reading science fiction, catching up on sleep ·

PAN DONGMING

Migrant restaurant worker
Shanghai

Monthly income (RMB) Personal – 650; Household – 650 · **Household budget (RMB)** Housing/Utilities – 0; Education – 0; Parent support – 400; Health care – 0; Food/Clothing/Other – 250; Savings – 0

每天早上八点就要起床，然后就是洗脸、刷牙乐，换上工作服之后就开始一天了。

首先就是～～大家的早饭问题。一个人切菜、一个人做饭、一个人做菜，总之，所有与早饭有关的事都是我的责任，也没有帮手。只有我一个人，一直忙到了九点了，大家也就陆陆续续起来了，我也就加快了我的脚步，不然到时间吃不上饭，挨骂的还是我。然后就只剩饭菜好了，那帮家伙便开始行动，毫不迟疑，而且速度快到可以用惊人来形容。——今天自然也不例外。

早饭吃粉丝，还是～我的老味。那帮家伙似乎还满意欢吃的，我只好先打好饭菜放在一边，不然等我把锅刷好出去的时候，可能就只剩下～～白白的米饭向我招手。而他们则开始收拾桌子了，我可不能再吃这样的饭了。饭都没吃上还说我动作慢，像老太婆，郁闷。

饭后没有休息就开始了上半天的工作。首先是打扫卫生，不过内部称之为"清理战场"，也就是扫扫地、擦擦台子，若是师父心血来潮的话，那还要～～得冲地了。不过人多好办事嘛，顶多二十分钟就可以搞定。然后又抽盘子，这才是最费力的差事。一看到架子上空空如也，我就知道，今天又有苦头吃了，果不虽然一下班就是半钟头，手都酸疼了还没得休息，还得加调料。不过这倒难不到我，想我好歹也干了一年了，这种小事还不是易如反掌，就连什么调料用多少、在什么地方，摆放的顺序等等我都驾轻就熟。

　　上午生意不景气啊，忙了一阵就只有休息了，其实休息也难受，坐也没地方坐，站着又累，还不如干活呢，唯一开心的就是大家可以开开玩笑，说些笑话之类的。

　　一点的时候竟然会停电，我的心情可以用狂喜来形容了吧，要不是场影响不好，我想我可能会放声大笑，哈哈，好久不容易停一次电啊，真可谓千年等一回，哈哈，不过还没高兴多久就来电了，只好继续战斗了。

　　午饭又是我烧，惯例了嘛，也没什么可说的，多做一点也不能怎么样，而且我的饭菜绝对是有我的特色的，土豆烧肉特色菜了，一看就知道是我烧的，我的土豆绝对是有特色，这一点就连师父们都不得不同意的，呵呵，主汤嘛，那是更有特色，不过这只是我一个人的观点，别人倒是没评价，大白菜切丝烧蛋汤，呵呵，就连我都有点奇怪，为什么汤全是蛋呢？想不通啊，一个个长得就跟蛋似的，还吃啊？！

173

PAN DONGMING'S DIARY

8:00 – Time to get up. I washed my face, brushed my teeth, and changed into my work uniform. The first thing I do is to make everyone's breakfast, so today I cut and cooked vegetables with rice noodles, just the way I like.

9:00 – Everyone else got up one by one, as usual. I always have to hurry. If I don't, people won't get breakfast on time, and I'll be in trouble. When the food was ready, the guys dove right in. They seemed to like my breakfast and ate amazingly fast. I had put some food aside for myself. Otherwise, by the time I did all the pots and pans, there would be nothing left for me but white rice.

9:30 – After that, we "cleared the battlefield," as we call it, which means sweeping the floor and cleaning the tables. Sometimes we have to mop the floor too, if the master chef suddenly decides we should. But it's not a big deal with so many of us. We finished in 20 minutes and then set the tables. That's a really hard job. It took half an hour of hard work today, and my arms were sore. We also arranged the spice bottles. I've gotten quite good at arranging them, knowing what spices aren't used very often, where to put them, and so on.

12:00 – Business wasn't very good this morning. We were busy for a short while and then got to rest. Actually, there isn't much rest to it because we don't have anything to sit on. So we stand around, and that's tiring. I'd rather be busy. The only good thing is that we get to joke around.

13:00 – A power outage – I was secretly ecstatic! I wanted to laugh out loud. But the power came back quickly, and I had to go back to work, this time to cook lunch for everyone. I didn't mind that – I'm getting pretty good after a year – but work in the afternoon was not so great. First, that guy Li didn't do a thing while the rest of us worked. Then we had an accident: I had forgotten the meat in the steamer.

By the time we took it out, it was too late. Even Master Yu, who is usually nice, was upset. It was my fault. Well, we were fortunate that nothing more serious happened. Otherwise, my meager salary would have been cut by at least half.

16:30 – We started to get busy, and the next four hours went by almost unnoticed. Except that my waist and back were both aching at the end.

21:00 – We finished cleaning, and I got to go home. Everyone else had to work another hour, just like I did in the morning. Alone in the dorm, I can't help thinking about how alone I am, so far away from home. But I have to do what I have to do. It's so different now. There, I did what I wanted, when I wanted to. What happy times!

A CHAT WITH PAN DONGMING

Where do you come from?
I was born in Sichuan province, but grew up in Guangxi province. I came to Shanghai because I couldn't find a job in Guangxi. I had graduated from middle school, but like most young people who live in rural areas, I didn't go on to high school.

How did you find this job?
My cousin helped me get it. There are about 20 workers, and I am the newest.

Do you get any time off?
Yes, we each get half a day off every week, and of course there's time after work. Then, I usually go out with friends for a while.

Where do you go?
We go to the Internet bar and chat on-line. That's how we get to know people. Some are old friends, some are new. Some are from work, and others are just people we play games with. Most of them have similar backgrounds and experience, similar living situations, and are about the same age. A few I chat on-line with every day. I wouldn't say I really know them, though. I only know them from what they've told me, so I'm not sure what's really true and what's not.

What do you chat about?
We talk about work, what kinds of jobs are better paid, easier to do, easier to get. Things like that. We also talk about the games we're playing on-line. You can't take the whole thing too seriously though. It's just for fun.

Do you look for girlfriends on-line?
No. Some friends of mine tried to find girlfriends on-line, but had no luck.

Do you read?

When I am bored. I was pretty difficult as a child, and my parents sometimes made me stay at home. So I read a lot, even novels, when there was nothing else. Now I like to read science fiction. I also collect Japanese cartoon cards, but they're really expensive.

Were you in middle school in Guilin in Guanxi province?

Yes. We were migrants, without resident status, so my parents had to pay 400 yuan tuition every semester for me. That was a lot of money, but they came up with it. I am their only child, after all.

What did your parents do for a living at that time?

They had a construction supplies business. When they arrived, they had to borrow money from relatives to start the business.

How was business then?

I worked with them for half a year. You got paid for what you sold. The worst was when we had no business for four months. We made nothing! But when it was good, it was really good. We sometimes made several hundred yuan a day – and one day we earned more than 3,000!

Are your parents still there?

No. They went back home to Sichuan last year. Like other Sichuanese, they like to play cards and chat with other people. So they wanted to go back.

Do you send them money?

Yes, I send 400 yuan a month, but my parents don't spend it. They're saving it for me. If I kept it here, I'm afraid nothing would be left at the end of my time here.

Do you call them often?

I'm not very homesick most of the time. When I started here, I didn't call for three months. Now I usually call them once a month on the public phone outside.

What's your plan for the future?

Frankly, I have no plan. People like us don't think much about the future. I need to focus on learning the skills I need now. I'm learning to cook both in the Sichuan and Shanghai style. The master chefs don't tell you how much salt, gourmet powder, or other ingredients to put in. You have to observe and experiment yourself.

How long will it take to become a master chef?

I'm not sure. One of the other guys here still hasn't become a master chef after three years.

Why not go to a cooking school?

I neither have time nor money. I look at this job as an apprenticeship.

When will you become a permanent staff member here?

Probably not this year. It usually takes one or two years. Our boss decides that. If there is an opening and you can do the job, it's yours. If there is no opening, you have to wait. Later, you can leave and open your own restaurant, but first you have to be sure that you really have the skills.

What do you think of Shanghai?

It's all right. But I haven't been out much. I came straight here to work once I arrived because I didn't have much money.

Are there any parts of Shanghai you're particularly interested in seeing?
I haven't thought about that. I haven't even figured out the names of the districts. Before I came, I knew nothing except that it was big and prosperous.

Are you happy here?
People in Shanghai are a little cold. In Guangxi, people meet in the street and can become friends in a matter of days. Here, it's hard to make friends. I have some, though, in the kitchen.

Does the restaurant provide you with medical insurance?
No. If I get sick, I have to take care of it myself. The restaurant covers only the master chefs. But we're usually fine.

THE FACTORY WORKER'S TALE
by Lin Chang-Zhi

It's not *what* you know in life that counts, but *who* you know.

What I know: I'm a graduate of the College of International Trade.

Who I know: My parents. It was through their "*who* you know" that I got a job in this state-owned factory. The factory is on the outskirts of Hefei City.

What I know: That was in 1998, a year after I graduated. 1998 was a bad year for international trade. Also for my parents. My father was 48 that year, which was when he got laid off. His separation package amounted to 10,000 yuan. For a life's work. At almost the same time, my mother's employer went bankrupt. It wasn't as if life had been easy for them before that. They had to pinch many pennies to put my sister and me through school.

Who I know: My father. He said that although my wages wouldn't amount to much, working in a state-owned factory would at least give me job security and a pension at the end.

What I know: I had no other options. As the words left my mouth to accept the job, I felt my young dreams slip away.

Who I know: The head of this enormous factory. Not personally, of course. He is said to have excellent connections in the city. This is how he is able to get so much financing.

What I know: I operate a large plastic-molding machine. It is foreign made, which is, I suspect, why I got assigned to it. I know a foreign language. I stand beside this machine every day and trim off the rough edges of the products as they come out. The leaders of the province and the city are impressed by the volume of machines like this. Volume is everything here, not profit. Because of this, banks are eager to finance increases in it. Once achieved, the volume impresses the leaders of the province and the city even more. To meet volume targets, we now work three shifts seven days a week. Recently, the factory got a loan to build an eight-story warehouse. We needed more space for all the volume that cannot be sold.

Who I know: My family. But they live far away in Bang-Pu.

What I know: I rent a furnished room on the outskirts of Hefei. On the morning shift, I get up at five, ride my bike to the factory, punch in, then dash out to the food stands at the factory gate for something to eat. I don't eat well. Food in the factory canteen has no taste. Management has a nice restaurant upstairs. Just the smells coming from it are more nourishing than what we get.

Who I know: Some porters. We ride home in the same direction at the end of the 2 p.m. shift. I ask them how they survive on 400 or 500 yuan a month. "What can we do?" they say, "We're lucky to have a job." But not giving weekends off is against labor and work regulations, I point out. You could sue them, I add. They tell me that someone did once, but nothing happened. The head of the factory has excellent connections.

Who I know: My father. He asked me, "What's your work like?"

What I know: We spend a lot of time trying to wangle the easiest job. How successful we are depends on who's the boss that day. For some, we have to work hard. With others, we can get away with murder. My father shook his head at this. In his day, they spent a lot of time trying to do a better job, he said. They worked with their bosses and ate with them, too.

Who I know: My workmates. Off shift we often hang out around the food stands. For 100 yuan, we'll get five or six spicy stir-fried dishes and a couple bottles of beer. We can't afford to go to bars or go dancing, so this is our limit. It's not so bad. Sometimes we play mahjong or cards, but for small stakes so that no one gets cleaned out.

What I know: Nothing pleases us more than a raise. I give almost all my pay to my parents, who are putting some aside for when I get married. None of us has money to burn. We buy the cheapest clothes and the cheapest cigarettes. I do buy expensive cigarettes occasionally, but only to hand around to friends. I don't want people to think I'm cheap.

Who I know: My former classmates at college. I play ping-pong and badminton with them. Lately, we've taken more to going to an Internet café. There we play on-line games.

What I know: When I'm in my room, I tend my plants and write. Like most of my workmates, I worry that I may never even meet a nice girl, let alone find one to marry. I know that only those who make the right friends get promoted at the factory. So, for me, my only hope is writing. It nurtures the dreams I have left – to have a wife and child. This is what I know.

Lin Chang-Zhi lives in Beijing. He is the author of "The Diary of the Sand Monk."

Age 33 · **Occupation** Factory worker in local electronics company in Zhongshan (Guangdong) · **Family** Wife, four-year-old daughter, mother · **Home** 100 m², four-bedroom, three-story townhouse · **Free time** Watching TV, listening to music, helping with homework, going to park with family ·

HE GUIQUAN

Factory worker
Guangdong

Monthly income (RMB) Personal – 1,000; Household – 2,300 (300 from his mother) · **Household budget (RMB)** Housing/Utilities – 300; Education – 400; Parent support – 0; Health care – n/a; Food/Clothing/Other – 1,200; Savings – 400

He Guiquan's Diary

7:00 – A new day … the weather had become warmer, and the sun was shining. I had 45 minutes to get ready for work. I washed, dressed, and ate the breakfast my wife had prepared. I watched TV for about ten minutes before leaving to check on the weather and get the news.

7:55 – I arrived at the factory, put away my bike, and punched in at 7:58 a.m., two minutes ahead of starting time. I chatted with my fellow workers for a while before starting my work, which is packaging.

11:30 – Before I knew it, it was time for lunch break. I hurriedly punched my card and went to the canteen with some of my friends. I dug into the food with terrific appetite because it was my favorite dish – sweet and sour pork ribs. Afterwards, I wandered around outside the factory and chatted with other workers.

14:00 – I started work again – the same thing I do every day – I watched the clock and looked forward to quitting time.

17:30 – Right after work, I left for the market near my home to pick up some things for dinner. I bought meat and fish, like I do every day, because my mother likes fish and my daughter likes meat. I bought a lot of food – cuttlefish, ham sausage, pork liver, ground meat, lettuce, Chinese cabbage, other vegetables, and more. It cost more than 50 yuan in all.

18:15 – I called out to my wife and daughter when I got home and asked them to take the things to the kitchen to prepare them. Soon everything was ready. We sat for about an hour as a family around the "hot pot."

19:15 – Afterwards, my wife washed the dishes and bathed our daughter, while I listened to music and watched the fish swimming in the fishbowl. Then my wife took her bath, and I took over caring for our daughter. This included helping her with her homework. When that was done, we watched a Hong Kong detective series on TV, as usual. My wife and I talk a lot while we're watching, mostly about what's going on in the program. Sometimes my daughter has comments too.

21:00 – We turned off the TV because my daughter had to go to bed. My wife and daughter always go to bed before I do. I went back downstairs to watch TV. I go to bed when I feel tired, which is usually around 11 p.m.

A CHAT WITH HE GUIQUAN

Your house is beautiful, just like townhouses in Shanghai.
You are so kind to say that! It now accommodates my whole family — my wife, my child, and my mother. My father is no longer alive. Since I am the youngest in my family, I inherited the house and the responsibility of taking care of my mother. That's our tradition. Here in Zhongshan we feel safer than in Guangzhou, except for around the railroad station, where there are a lot of people from outside the area. I know my neighbors very well here, so I don't even bother to lock the door.

What do you and your wife do for a living?
We both work at an electronics plant. That's also where we met. The factory makes TVs. I used to do electrical soldering. Now I do packaging, which is lighter work. My wife is an accountant there.

Do workers make a good salary there?
We each earn around 1,000 yuan a month.

What kinds of benefits does your factory provide?
The firm deducts a small amount each month to cover medical insurance for serious illness. We pay for minor ailments out of our own pockets. The company also has a pension plan, which gives you several hundred yuan a month after retirement. My job is very secure, although the pay is not that great. I expect to keep the job until I retire at 50.

You mentioned your daughter is in kindergarten. When did she start?
At three. Later she will go to elementary school, which will be cheaper than kindergarten, about 600 yuan per year.

What is your daughter's favorite pastime?
She is a big fan of foreign cartoons. So we buy a lot of DVDs for her.

188

She also likes to go on walks with us. We know that an only child can be lonely without brothers or sisters, but we can't afford to have a second one: We could be fined more than 100,000 yuan.

What level of education do you expect your daughter to achieve?
She should have a senior high school education, I think. Given the popularity of college education these days, she might even go on to college. I hope she can make it on her own merits because it won't be possible for me to afford overseas study unless I win the lottery. If she could go to college in Guangzhou, it would be great; if she could go to college in Beijing, it would be a miracle. But we are not very ambitious. We just want a stable life.

Are there any migrant workers in your factory?
It used to be all locals here, but the number of migrant workers is increasing. Migrant workers make less than we do. They take jobs that normally pay 1,000 yuan, but they settle for 700. And they work much longer hours than we do too.

What do you think of migrant workers?
Frankly, I look down upon them. They are impolite and they have even less education than people like us. Also, they certainly cost us locals  many jobs. But I also see that our economy here needs them. They take the most unattractive jobs in Zhongshan, like road construction work, and will work for 400 or 500 yuan a month. And they don't get medical benefits or retirement pensions because they're not permanent employees. It's still better for them than in their home towns, where they can do nothing but work on a farm. They are not very happy, I guess, though you can't really tell that from the way they act.

Do local workers get along with migrant workers at your factory?

We don't have much contact, since we basically live and work separately. We are only in contact with a few of the more skilled ones. Besides, dialects create barriers for both sides. We all speak our own dialects, not Mandarin. We don't have much conflict, since we don't really communicate.

What do you think of all the changes in China?

The changes have been dramatic. In the 1980s, we got running water – a nice change from having to carry water from the river. In those days we used to own plots of land where we grew rice and vegetables. When I was 11 or 12, we were told that town residence cards were available for sale. So we sold our land and bought residence status. I regretted that decision later because the land we sold was used for a new factory. It's making good profits today, while we get nothing. Yes, China has come a long way. We used to heat our stoves with straw, then it was wood. By the 1990s, we had gas. We even have electric boilers now. People's attitudes have changed too. Many people go abroad to study, and some of my friends even married foreigners. The whole country is much more open-minded. But the big changes have also brought new pressures.

What kinds of pressure?

For me, I have more family pressures as the breadwinner these days. I used to be carefree as the youngest in the family, but now I am the

one who shoulders most of the burden of supporting my mother. If my mother needs medical treatment, my brothers and sisters will cover some of the costs if I can't handle it alone. My biggest concern now is my mother's health. A serious illness is very, very expensive.

Do you follow national events in the newspapers or on TV?

I am not interested in national events. I watch TV, but I don't read the papers.

Are you interested in what foreign countries are doing?

I get to know the outside world through TV since I can't afford to travel abroad. From the TV, I know that people in the U.S. live in comfortable conditions – even beggars have a decent life. If I could leave Zhongshan and live somewhere else, I'd definitely go to America. My second choice would be Japan. We also learn about other countries through entertainment shows,  ones about Japanese or Korean celebrities and that kind of thing. We can go on a package tour to Hong Kong, too, which is not far away. I've been to Macau myself.

Where else do you want to visit?

I want to go to Beijing. I went to Shanghai 15 years ago after the metro had just opened. Travel inside China is not that expensive anymore. A four-day trip to Beijing, including flight, lodging and food, costs only 1,000 yuan.

THE RETIRED FARMER'S TALE
by An Chang-He

September 29th is an important anniversary for Laodu. Yet he sleeps late. If, out of habit, he reproaches himself about getting up so late, he very soon comes to his own defense. He asks himself what else is there to do these days but sleep. His wife is gone. His children are gone. His land is gone.

It was ten years ago on this day that Laodu's wife died. When his wife was first told she had cervical cancer, the doctors advised her to have a complete hysterectomy. She refused. "My womb," she said, "has produced two sons and two daughters. It is strong, and I am keeping it." The doctors couldn't dissuade her. She told Laodu that a woman without a womb is no longer a woman. By the time Laodu convinced her that she would always be woman enough for him, it was too late. The doctors told them there was no more point in operating.

Once his wife was buried, Laodu was free — 57 and totally free. Free of everything. The last of his land had been expropriated for a factory. His younger son had moved far away to Guangzhou as soon as he graduated from university. One of his daughters had married a man in Hong Kong, and the other had moved to Beijing.

The twin daughters used to be the "apples of his eye". Neighbors and relatives were often envious of their having twins, especially two such pretty girls. Their beauty had been a double-edged sword, though. They had been more concerned about their looks than their schooling. Both had gone on to become fashion models. When Laodu first saw them walking down the catwalk swinging their hips, his face flushed with shame.

But the twins do send money regularly. When they first started doing this, he hadn't known how to react. He'd never had so much money at one time. All his life, Laodu had lived frugally. Of course he was pleased that they were both doing well, but it was almost as if they wanted to embarrass him, he thought. He spent days looking at the wad of notes in his hand, trying to think how he could possibly spend it. In the end, he decided to keep a third of it for his own needs and to send the rest to his older son. He called those two-thirds his "conscience money."

In the early years after Laodu and his wife were allotted the farm, they did very well selling their vegetables. When Laodu saw he needed help with the work, he kept his son home from school, while the others sent their sons to school. Over time, as the city began to outgrow its boundaries, they began to lose their land, piece by piece. Gradually, his son did not have enough to live on and moved to the city to start a business.

At the beginning, his son had seemed to prosper in the city. He wore nice clothes and had all the latest conveniences. But then he started speculating on the stock market. Laodu wondered why so many others had been able to make a small fortune this way, while his son lost everything. The fault, Laodu decided, had to be his. He had deprived him of a proper education.

On this slow-starting anniversary day, Laodu has a late breakfast of thin egg noodles and takes his medicine. He doesn't own a clock or a watch. As a farmer he had let the season and the weather govern his day. Now he turns his head attentively. He hears exercise music being piped out of the loudspeaker at the nearby school. This means it must be almost noon. He hurries to the store to buy incense and candles. This he had meant to do the day before, but he had been unable to get away from Laolin.

Laolin, three years younger than Laodu, had been a farmer like him, but not as lucky. Not as lucky with his children, nor with his farm. When everyone else was growing vegetables, Laolin grew only grains, which never got a very good price. But he had worried that if he weren't successful selling vegetables, he wouldn't have any rice to eat. By the time Laolin realized his mistake and switched to vegetables, the city had taken so much of his land that he couldn't make a living on it. These days Laolin has hardly enough to eat, wears old, beat-up clothes, and has cancer of the liver in the final stages. Hearing the bad news about his health, Laodu had felt he could not just turn away and go on with his errands.

Today, as he starts tidying up around his wife's grave, he apologizes for being so late on this day. He hadn't been there for a year, and the gravesite had become overgrown. In the first year after her death, he used to come nearly every day. But the intervals between his visits gradually lengthened, until he came only on Qingming, the anniversary of her death. "It's not because I don't want to come," he tells her. He's still kneeling where he has been pulling up weeds. "It's the walk. It takes me three hours back and forth now. The hill is so steep. If I'd have known it would take me this long I'd have had you buried next to my bed." He sighs. "Not that you'd be very safe there. It looks like ours is the next house to be torn down. For more factories, I assume. I guess there won't be any farms or any farmers left here at all soon."

He pushes himself to his feet and starts to go. But he can't say goodbye to her with such depressing thoughts like that. So he puts on a teasing face. "I've been introduced to a woman," he tells her. "She used to be an opera singer with the Sichuan Opera, and you know how I like the Sichuan Opera. She's a good-looking woman and was interested in me, but I had to turn her down ..." Laodu sees he can't keep up the pretence: "I didn't want her to catch what I've got," he added. "I felt something a few days ago in my chest and went to have it checked. It's bad, they said. I haven't told the children. I don't want to bother them. They're all so busy. But don't you be sad, Dearie. I'll be with you soon." As he goes back down the hill, Laodu has to stop to catch his breath every few steps. The brilliant evening sun is piercing. Squinting, he tries to see where the city ends and the fields begin.

An Chang-He has published over a hundred novels, novellas, and short stories, including "Rat and Man," "Meat Rice," and "The X Report."

Age 41 · **Occupation** Shop owner in Zhongshan (Guangdong) · **Family**
Husband, 11-year-old daughter · **Home** Two condominiums, each 80-90 m² ·
Free time Helping with daughter's homework · **Monthly income (RMB)**

FENG CHANGMING

Shop owner
Guangdong

Personal – 5,000; Household – 5,000 · **Household budget (RMB)** Housing/
Utilities – 600; Education – 400; Parent support – 500; Health care – 1,000;
Food/Clothing/Other – 1,000; Savings – 1,500

2008年12月9日. 星期五. 晴.

　　好不容易又到了周末. 早晨6:00. 手机闹钟不停的连续响起, 使我从睡梦中惊醒. 习惯的用手擦之眼睛. 很不情愿的穿衣起床. 感觉今天的天气比起昨两天要暖和多了. 顺手打开电视机看之. 温度已回升至最高01度. (回想昨两天最高温度才有12度左右). 着过后. 急着梳洗一番. 后习惯穿上运动鞋去门热身一番. 到公园跑上一大圈后. 已是7:00点. (生命在于运动). 接着到就近的金冠路馆买了一些早点. 就忙着往家里赶. 家里还有了大的和小的在睡懒觉. 今天没那么冷还不快起床……

　　女儿叫之吵之起床洗刷一遍. 就用之与顺手拿了她最爱的三文治. 蛋煮皮牛奶. 边吃边喝. 过后马上穿上袜子鞋子. 背起书包上学. 送了女儿上学后. 我也赶上班. 老公去开铺.

　　今天是周五. 需要把一周的工作资料整理归纳核实一下. 及新来的产品及规划分类那些单位需要送货都作好安排. 早两天天气较冷. 出行的人比较稀少. 生意也受到一定影响. 今天天气回暖. 生意也有所上升. 转眼已到下午11:30. 也要到学校接小孩. 放学的时间. 到校飞赶上小孩放学. 迎面看见孩之位张老师. 顺便和她招手及谈了一些关于女儿学习的好坏等. 马上要结束这学期. 1月11号星期一开始大考. 1月14号放寒假.

时间地转学，张老师还特别分时要加强关注小孩的各方面的发展，并相对来说女儿的学习成绩，特别是数语英三科有明显的进步，作为家长的我听老师名夸女儿，心里感到欣慰。还有下学期就要升中的女儿来说也是件很关键的问题，不过也将顺其自然，不能给太大的压力……谈着谈着，已到12点分，张老师也该下班了，今天后送女儿回辅，先生也做好早饭，中午一般都是先生做饭，饭后有时看之书，看之报纸（中山简报），至中午11点分又要送小孩上学了。通常由我送，但近段时间，由于家里在装修，基本上都是大丈夫送女儿上学后再到家里跟之装修的事项，铺找由我一人看管，本来铺里有了2人，由于上有了同地回家生小孩，暂时还没上班，因此由两口子打理，家族小生意，况且做我们这一行，请人也不是那么容易，一些要对这行专业也才可以做，有节日时过不过来，小心也可以帮忙。

　　下午基本了：30接女儿放学，6：00上市场买菜回家做晚饭，但由于这段时间家里装修有时都没时间做晚饭，干脆到外边简粗之的三菜一汤，花上一句心十之也就解决一号了。

　　晚上7：30会回到家，丈夫第一时间打开电视，看中央之大记演8：00，TV剧之吧，9：00 珠江电视台"今日关注"节目，点上之间（大约11：30洗好睡床，一天的辛苦也到了休息的时间……

FENG CHANGMING'S DIARY

6:00 – The alarm clock rang. I rubbed my eyes, yawned, and reluctantly got out of bed. It was Friday, so at least the weekend was practically here. I turned on the TV and saw that today would be warmer, as high as 21°C. After washing and dressing, I put on my running shoes and went out to warm up for my run.

7:00 – I finished my run in the park. (I can't live without exercise!) Then I walked over to the bakery nearby to buy some things for breakfast. I ran back home with my things and woke up my husband and daughter. She got right up and I washed with her. She ate her favorite sandwich, some cake, and had a glass of milk. After she finished, she put on her shoes and socks, and I took her to school. Meanwhile, my husband went to open the shop.

8:00 – At the shop, I did the paperwork for the week, put some merchandise on the shelves, and made arrangements for a couple of deliveries. It had been cold the past few days, so fewer people had been out shopping. That affected our business, but now it was warmer and business would be better.

11:30 – While picking up my daughter at school, I ran into her class teacher. She told me to pay special attention right now because exams were coming up, and it was crucial for my daughter to go on to middle school. She said my daughter had made great progress in Chinese, Mathematics, and English this term, which I was very happy to hear. I agree that she should continue her education, but as her mother, I don't want to put too much pressure on her. It's better just to let nature take its course.

12:00 – My husband made lunch for us, which he usually does. After lunch, we read for a while. We normally read books like Jin Yong's Kung Fu fiction or the Zhongshan business newspaper.

13:45 – My husband took our daughter back to school. He has been doing this often recently because he needs to go back home to discuss the renovation of our apartment with the workers. I stay at the shop. We used to have a helper in the shop, but she went home to have a baby two months ago. Now we run the shop by ourselves. It's not easy to find someone to help because it's really a small family business. And only people with specialized knowledge can do the job. My daughter sometimes gives us a hand when we are extremely busy, like on holidays.

17:30 – I picked up my daughter and went to the fresh market to buy some things for dinner.

18:30 – At home, I cooked dinner for the three of us. (Recently, we've gone out to dinner a lot because of the remodeling work.) After dinner, my husband watched TV – the "Chinese Art Grand Performance," "TV Film Club," and "Today's Focus." After that, he surfed the Internet for a while, then we took a bath together.

23:30 – To bed at the end of a long, tiring day!

A CHAT WITH FENG CHANGMING

When did your family return to China from Indonesia?
My parents came back in 1960, and I was born in 1964. My husband's family also re-immigrated to China from Indonesia.

Did your family suffer during the Cultural Revolution?
Not too much, because we completely broke off contact with our relatives in Indonesia. Otherwise, we would have been risking our lives. It was even dangerous to send or receive letters. But it was a bad time. People didn't trust anyone; people disappeared.

How long have you been running your incense and candle shop?
Almost eight years. I had graduated from college in Economics and was working as a manager in a textile mill when it was privatized in

1998, so I got laid off. With a little savings, the separation package, and some loans from relatives and friends, I opened this shop. I didn't know a lot about incense or candles, but my father-in-law was very knowledgeable about idol worship, and for idol worship, you need incense and candles. My husband joined me in the business later, after he lost his job as a construction company manager. We both enjoy the freedom of owning our own business.

Do you have any employees?
We used to have a woman who helped out, but she went back home to have a baby. You need people with quite a bit of knowledge in this business. If your customer wants to worship Guanyin (the Goddess of Mercy), for instance, you would be in big trouble if you gave him the incense for worshipping Guangong (a famous ancient general).

How is business these days?
Just so-so. It's the off-season, so we take in a couple thousand yuan per

month. But during Chinese New Year and other festivals, we may take in over 10,000 yuan a month. We've been able to pay back all of the 100,000 yuan we invested, and we can easily cover all our living expenses.

Have you ever thought about expanding your business?
Yes. Right now the shop is about 20 m², and as you can see, it's completely packed. My husband wants to make it into a chain, but good shop assistants are hard to find. Plus our child is still young. We may wait on this.

Who are the typical buyers of incense and candles?
Most are retail customers. You can see an idol at nearly every door here in Zhongshan. Some business customers also place large orders for Chinese New Year. Idol worship is very popular here and always has been. Even during the Cultural Revolution people would light incense secretly.

You live in two apartments, I understand.
Yes, one where we've been living for more than ten years and another, which is new. We don't want to cook in the new apartment because we don't want it smoky. So we eat in the old one and sleep in the new one, sort of as if we were on vacation.

How about living expenses?
We don't have to spend a lot on our daughter's tuition, but the extra review courses she goes to on Saturdays cost over 1,000 yuan each term. I also invest in the stock market, and that's been quite profitable. I only buy low-risk stocks that show good performance, and I also buy bonds, which yield more than banks can offer. So I don't have much cash lying around in my bank account.

Where did you learn all that?

I learned a lot from former colleagues. When business is good, we can save and invest thousands of yuan a month. But we also spend a lot. We spend thousands on health insurance and my parents' medical bills. We also give financial support to other children in the family.

Is it hard to find time to be with your daughter?

My husband and I take turns looking after her, but she is 11. Right now she seems more interested in our business than in her school work. I think she has a talent for it.

Do you hope your daughter will run the business with you some day?

We'll let her decide that for herself. She helps out during the busy times and gets a lot of praise from customers. She told me she would look after the shop for me during her school breaks.

How is she doing with her schoolwork?

 I will put a little pressure on her there. If she passes the entrance exams, I'll do all I can to support her, even if I have to borrow. But I won't buy her way through. If your exam score isn't high enough to qualify for the best schools or universities, you can pay to get in. If you've got 50,000 yuan, you can get into the best middle school in town, but I won't do that. She has to make it on her own merit.

Have you ever thought about sending her abroad for further study?

No. We're all here, and we would worry if she went abroad. After all, she's our only child. It's true that she could get a better degree abroad, but she might decide to stay there after graduation like so many do. I want her to stay here with us.

What do you think of all the changes China has been going through?
Policies are always in flux. Take the one-child policy, for example. You get fined 80,000 yuan if you have a second child today. But some people do it anyway. Back when we were state employees, you would have been fired instead, and nobody could afford that in those days.

What do you do in your free time?
I don't watch TV very often, but my husband watches a lot – entertainment, cartoons, news. He is very interested in current affairs, while I don't know much about these things. He is also keen on basketball and soccer. He can talk with his friends about ball games for hours at a time. I don't have time for TV. We work all day, and when I get home, there's housework, cooking, and helping my daughter with homework. My husband rarely gives me a hand with these things.

What are your concerns about the future?
I have no major worries. I'm quite satisfied with my life now. The only little worry is my husband wanting to buy a car. I'm afraid he might spend too much time riding around with friends and not enough time working at the shop. But I'm in charge of the money, so he'll have to wait until I agree.

Age 35 · **Occupation** Department head, Government Bureau for Public Complaints, disguised location · **Family** Husband · **Home** 140 m², three-bedroom condominium · **Free time** Listening to music, gardening, dining out, traveling, reading work-related literature · **Monthly income (RMB)** Personal –

MRS. WU

Department head, Government Bureau for Public Complaints
Disguised location

2,000; Household – 5,000 · **Household budget (RMB)** Housing/Utilities – 1,000; Education – 0; Parent support – 1,000; Health care – n/a; Food/Clothing/Other – 1,000; Savings – 2,000

7:30　老公的手机闹铃响了起

7:45　我的"米老鼠"闹钟也响了，伸出一只手，昨天
　　　们天气预报讲今天会有寒潮，果然，气温下
　　　降了不少，赖在被里不想起来，心里想今天
　　　可以不上班该有多好，看看表7:50分了，看来
　　　是不能睡懒觉自然醒了．　　　（我不喜欢这样冷的冬天，还
　　　　　　　　　　　　　　　　　　　　　　　是北国的冬天：白雪皑皑、冰情回溅、
7:53分　果断的一次定以最快的速度起了床……　童话般的景物
　　　　　　　　　　　　　　　　　　　　　　　　……

7:57分　放CD音乐（舒伯特小夜曲）洗早餐（昨晚
　　　在小区放超市买的牛奶、窝头．）

8:05分　话音陪伴、餐桌上那些丰盛的早餐，试
　　　　了试老公出差带回来了那些蛋糕，真好．（香味
　　　不错，有些香草的水果味．）

8:10分　老公带好手表、准备出门．我提醒他天气
　　　太冷，多穿点……　老公出门到
　　　小飞楼下等公车（路程大约1小时）

8:15分　我准备出门　（把报箱里的报纸拿进屋
　　　摆进家，我订的《参考》、时报，此报内容值得我强。

8:20分　带上手表、准备路上吃（馒头＋鸡蛋＋牛奶）

8:20分　在小区楼下坐单位的交通车（我住的公交谈话区）
　　　　有时没有交通车就坐"的士"或公交车（"的士"
　　　　车到单位车费14元，公交车1元，坐的还比较舒服。
8:30分　上车，听MP3音乐，到办公室大约需20分钟
　　　　左右。

9:00分　到单位上班。
9:10分　开始学习《XX市长关于城市第十一个五年规划建议》
10:30分　到接待室大厅看一看今天接洽咨询的是哪
　　　　一个律师事务所的律师，然后就基本
　　　　依据当事人就有关具体问题进行
　　　　探讨。（为了配合2005年5月国务院颁
　　　　布的信访条例的实施，XX市司法
　　　　局指派每天有一个律师事务所的律师来信访接
　　　　待室进行公益心的的法律、法规咨
　　　　询。(就是说不开始就都通过一些方法引导
　　　　去着此xxxxxx查询一些相关xxxx反映问题
　　　　　　　　　　　　　　　　　　合法的

11:00　到办公室学习《信访条例》
11:30　处理昨天接待过的一个上访群众的文件材料，
　　　xxx接接待接待处处理。

Mrs. Wu's Diary

7:30 – The alarm went off – first my husband's portable, then my Mickey Mouse clock.

8:00 – I put on a CD and made breakfast with steamed bread, egg, and milk and packed it for each of us to take to work. Then I washed and put some nice lotion on my face. I also dabbed on some of the new perfume my husband gave me. Before he left for work, I reminded him to dress warmly. It was going to be cold. He left to catch the bus, which gets him to work in about an hour. I went out to pick up the city newspaper from our box. It's a readable paper.

8:30 – I left with my breakfast in hand and ate it on the Bureau's shuttle bus on my way to work. (We live in the neighborhood reserved for civil servants). I listened to some music on my MP3 player on the bus.

9:00 – I arrived at the office and started looking at the 11th Five-Year Plan for the City, which was just issued by the mayor.

10:30 – I went to the reception to find out what lawyers were on duty today and then discussed a few matters with one of them. (The government has begun to realize the need to provide legal counsel to the public, so the city appoints private lawyers on a rotating basis to do this for our petitioners.) I went to the reference library to review the "Public Information Act."

12:00 – I had lunch in the canteen. Today I had kelp soup, braised fish in brown sauce, fried greens, and cabbage salad. I took a 30-minute nap on the sofa in my office. Afterwards, I went to a nearby supermarket to buy groceries for dinner – fish, eggplant, greens, and ground meat.

14:00 – Back at the office, I logged onto the city's intranet to search for some information and read some files. I wish we had an Internet link. Then we would have access to more information and could explain more about the laws and policies to the public. I always feel under pressure at work because it seems I never have enough information. Then I met with people from a nearby district to help settle a dispute between property owners and a developer.

17:00 – With the day's work done, I chatted with some colleagues about "The Promise," a new hit movie directed by Chen Kaige. I felt it was a mixture of commercialism, hi-tech production, and elements borrowed from popular American films.

17:30 – I took the shuttle bus home.

18:00 – I started preparing dinner – spicy fish (my husband's favorite), eggplant with meat, stir-fried potatoes, and pumpkin soup. My husband came home soon after and watched TV until dinner was ready. We ate together. (We have no children but are planning for one now.) My husband has been very busy lately because a Brazilian customer was demanding higher product quality. He is impressed by the Brazilians' entrepreneurial spirit and said we Chinese could learn a lot from them.

19:30 – My husband washed the dishes and chopsticks and cleaned up the kitchen. I went to the balcony to water the flowers.

20:00 – I watched the CCTV news. Then my husband watched soccer, which I don't enjoy, so I went to the kitchen and made a fruit milk tea from a recipe I found. He said it was better than the tea he'd had in western restaurants. I called my parents since I haven't had time to visit them lately. Everything was fine with them. We both talked with my in-laws and invited them to visit us this weekend.

21:30 – Our neighbor, who is a doctor, came by to see us. We talked about bird flu, and she suggested some precautions.

22:00 – After she left, I washed up and went to bed at 10:30 p.m.

A CHAT WITH MRS. WU

Your apartment is very nice. How long have you lived here?
Two years. Every city government staff member is eligible to buy a government-subsidized apartment. The size varies according to your position. I paid 1,000 yuan per square meter, but the apartment is actually worth three times that. I was also able to use my housing insurance to get a low-interest mortgage, which most of my colleagues at work did as well.

What department do you work in?
The Bureau for Public Complaints. I'm the department head. We are  responsible for responding to inquiries from all the districts of the city. Every day, one staff member is in charge of dealing directly with the people. When we meet with them or get letters or calls, the first thing we do is determine whether the issue is covered by a policy. If it is, we try to get something done for them. If not, we notify the appropriate organization and request assistance.

What are the most common problems you encounter?
There are all kinds. Sometimes people even come to you for help with family arguments. They think the government is there to take care of everything. But we encounter serious problems as well, like when a farmer's land is expropriated or a state-owned company is privatized and workers get laid off.

What can you do for people with such problems?
I explain the current policy. It's mainly a matter of communication. If the owner of private land comes to us with a grievance, we try to help him or her get the proper compensation. Our job is to communicate the interests of the public at large to the leaders of city government.

Do people usually feel better after receiving your explanation?

I help wherever I can. But if I'm unable to help solve the problem, at least I can explain the policy to them. Compensation for the loss of private land is very low, for example, but that's the policy. We can't change it simply because we feel sorry for them. We're going through a period of great change. The old problems are still around, and new ones come up all the time – welfare, urbanization, transportation, loss of land, to name a few. We just try to be human in the face of it all.

It seems that your job demands a solid grasp of policies and regulations. What is your background?

The entry qualifications for this job are not that high, and there were none at all until this year. Many people don't believe that local administrative organizations like ours can solve their problems. They think all the qualified officials are in Beijing. That's the way it used to be, but responsibility has been given to us to relieve pressure there. Premier Wen has emphasized the importance of our work, and that has led to more demanding job requirements. I didn't study law. I was trained as a secretary, and many of my colleagues came from the army. They were trained  to follow strict military procedures and haven't learned to respond quickly with practical solutions. So we have also recruited several college graduates during the past two years. There are now seven people in my department, two of whom have studied law and one who came to us via the civil service exam process. My staff is generally older, 50 and up. Only one is still in his 20s. At 35, I'm relatively young for a department head.

What career aspirations do you have?

My supervisor has talked to me about this. He said I have great promise as a female employee at my age. But I'm not really ambitious. I'm satisfied if I can help people solve their problems. Leaders can't know everything about everyone, so communication flows through intermediaries. I feel under a lot of pressure right now because I'm not trained in law. My strengths are my life experience and my strong desire to learn. As soon as a new law or regulation comes out, I buy it at the bookstore and read it.

How do you know when there is a new law or regulation?

My job puts me in contact with all kinds of people, and sometimes they know more about the law than I do. I have no problem admitting I don't know something – it's not a matter of losing face. But if we had better training and access to information, we would be better able to anticipate problems and respond more effectively, I think.

What kind of training are you getting now?

None. I have to buy all my books. We can't even access the Internet, where many policies are publicized. This is partly due to lack of funding, but a lot has to do with the mindset of our leaders. All they seem to want is for us to get the petitioners to go back home. You know about that resort developed by that big developer? Residential buildings were torn down already 13 years ago to make way for it, but the people who lived there are still waiting for compensation. We've tried to put some  pressure on the responsible authorities, but all we can do is talk to them. We often say that we are nothing but a bunch of tongues in our department. Perhaps I take all of this too seriously, but working here for two years has made me very tired. If I took another job, I think things would be easier and I would be happier.

Are you planning to join the Communist Party?

I don't want to join, but my supervisor keeps suggesting it. We've even quarreled about it. One of my colleagues told me his supervisor also wanted him to join the Party, but he said he would join only when it has been cleaned up. Maybe we've seen too much of the dark side of the Communist Party.

What about corruption?

It's very widespread. Even leaders who urge us to cultivate ethical behavior are sometimes taking money under the table. Bribes can run into the millions. Functional departments with decision-making authority often sell their decisions. Even ordinary citizens know it's going on, and they are losing their trust in the law. Often, the things they ask for are very reasonable, but the law just isn't on their side. Some of my friends have gone abroad and tell me how good things are in foreign countries. Actually, I think conditions here in a material sense are not bad. What we lack are good laws and the will to obey them. If a country wants to prosper, it needs sound rules that people can follow. I would say that the country has a real deficit in this area.

What is your income as a government clerk?

It's about average in the department, about 2,000 yuan a month. If my husband didn't earn what he does, we wouldn't be able to live so comfortably. I've worked in the government for more than ten years. The house is the only benefit I get.

What do you and your husband do in your free time?

My husband has no free time. He's in charge of sales and works from morning till night and on weekends too. So I spend a lot of time alone. I like to sleep late on Saturdays and Sundays. I enjoy listening to music and tending my flowers. I cook at night for us, and I visit my parents once a month. Of the few friends I have, some are already retired. We spend time together eating and chatting. My job has changed my personality, I think. I enjoy my peace and quiet, just like an old woman.

What do you do in your quiet time?

I sit in this chair and listen to music on my MP3 player. I'm mentally exhausted. Everybody talks about harmony, but we certainly don't have it as public servants. I spend most of my time in the office listening to complaints. People often use us to vent their anger. Once, a man came in with a gun. I called my supervisor in, and the man hid the gun in his sleeve. People aren't happy with the government, and they have no other way to express their anger. We are the ones who deal directly with them, but we don't get enough support, morally or materially.

Yet you seem like a very calm person. Do you have much vacation?

I get two weeks a year. But I never take it. Asking for vacation is a sign of immaturity or laziness in many people's minds, but I think you should be able to take it if you're entitled to it. The best solution would be to make vacation compulsory. People need rest and recreation. It would help them be better employees.

You seem to have a strong marriage.

We love each other. We live in harmony. We don't have a child yet. We are good friends, and our financial situation is also not bad. We've already paid off the mortgage, and we go out to dinner a lot. If I see some clothes I like, I buy them. It's not a hardship to save. And with my government pension, we don't have to worry about our retirement.

THE TALE OF THE HYDRAULIC WORKER
by Liu Fang

Part I

Yang Jian-Jun wakes up with a jolt. It is 7 a.m. The washing machine is wheezing and gurgling like an old man washing up at the sink. Even louder, he thinks. Then it begins to roar, then whine like a jet engine. No hope of getting back to sleep. He reaches for his cigarettes. The pack is empty. Then he remembers the pack of White Sand he was given yesterday. A worker like him may be given many things, but rarely a pack of White Sand. Where were they anyway?

Hearing him moving about, his wife comes into the bedroom. She starts taking off the bedding. "Where's my White Sand?" he asks her. "Oh, not only do they stink, but they've made this quilt stink too," she grumbles. "Where are they? I gave them away! A poor worker like you shouldn't be smoking a cigarette like White Sand."

Yang Jian-Jun fills his lungs with air to yell, but thinks better of it. Fingering the 5-yuan bill deep in his trouser pocket, he asks her instead for money for cigarettes. She turns from the washing machine and glares at him. "I've given you 300 yuan already this week. Where did it go?" He tells her he used it to pay the water and electricity bills. "Ha! No way did that cost 300 yuan. You lost it gambling, you good-for-nothing!"

At that moment, their daughter comes in to ask for money. "Ask your father! I don't have any!" Standing there half-dressed in front of his child, Yang Jian-Jun feels once again he's been made to be a fool.

Part II

His daughter has been given the day off from school to visit her grandmother in the hospital. She needs money for her fare. Yang Jian-Jun sees he can't give her his 5 yuan with his wife still standing there, not after having just told her he's broke. So he finishes dressing and walks into the cycle shop next door. He borrows 500 yuan from the

218

owner, who is his friend. That tucked away, he goes back to the house. He pulls the crumpled 5-yuan bill out of his pocket and gives it to his daughter. Yang Jian-Jun congratulates himself on his little deception and goes back to chat with his friend at the shop.

His wife, passing by the shop as she leaves for work, is not fooled. She gives him one of her false smiles. Yang Jian-Jun decides to stay out of her way for the rest of the day. But the day is still young. He decides to go to the market for some spring onions. He will chop them up and put them in the fish soup he will make for his sick mother-in-law. In the market, the girl in the vegetable stall calls to him: "Boss Yang!" Being called "Boss" gives him a very pleasant feeling of importance. "Give me some spring onions," he tells the girl. "Want some fish to go with them?" she asks. "You're some saleslady," he tells her, and makes a show of looking through his pockets. "What a shame, I don't seem to have enough on me." "Never mind," she smiles her blessed smile, "Next time."

Part III
Waiting for Yang Jian-Jun back at his house is Young Liu. He is also a hydraulic worker, but a college graduate who has been assigned to work with him. Their task today is to inspect the irrigation ditches belonging to the Village of Dragon Spring. This month – September – is the easiest time of the year for Yang Jian-Jun. Last year's flood-and-drought prevention works are all completed, and the inspection of local projects has not yet gotten into full swing.

Yang Jian-Jun drives his motorcycle to the village with Young Liu on the back. They work for two hours inspecting the irrigation ditches and tell the nervously waiting village officials that it doesn't look too bad at all, not much needs to be done. These welcome words get them an invitation to the home of the Party Secretary, the most powerful man in the village. They will be treated as honorable guests.

In his garden, several turtles, just caught in the pond, are added to an already aromatic stew. The tender meat of young chickens has been stir-fried with soy sauce, and the rice is so fragrant that Yang Jian-Jun has two helpings. The eggs they crack to add to the grain alcohol drink are so fresh they are still warm. There are toasts made to the honorable hydraulic workers, again and again. They get an invitation to go fishing. Young Liu would go, but Yang Jian-Jun says that he must visit his mother-in-law in the hospital.

This is when, with tongues loosened by their drink, the teasing begins. "We heard your mother-in-law is a college lecturer ... what did your wife see in you?" "We heard you beat your wife ... and she hasn't left you yet?" Aware of his responsibility as host, the Village Secretary slowly rolls a cigarette and delivers his opinion: "A husband's pride must never be undermined. Once a woman marries a man, her lot is in his hands."

Part IV
On the phone with his daughter: "Lin? Ask your Gran for her house key so I can cook some fish soup for her." His daughter transfers the message: "Gran, Dad wants your house key ... wants to make you some soup ... to cook it at your house." Yang Jian-Jun now hears his mother-in-law's voice clearly in the background: "Tell him 'No'! He'll only make a mess!"

Part V
Behind Yang Jian-Jun's one-story house, there is a vegetable patch and a small pond. In the afternoon, the garden gets very warm. Slipping his hand into the still cool pond with a skill born of practice, Yang Jian-Jun catches a carp by its tail fin and slaps it onto the chopping board he has laid on the ground. He is pretty sure he is the only man in town who can catch a fish like this.

The glow of pride rapidly fades as he looks over at his motorcycle. He has told his friend, the cycle shop owner, to sell it for him, but not for less than 3,000 yuan. He wants to buy his daughter a computer. He has already seen the perfect one. The money from the motorcycle will cover most of it, so he will have to borrow the rest. His wife is dead set against his plan, but his daughter is so keen on it. That his daughter sought and found an ally in him makes him determined to win the endless marital war he and his wife wage daily. Just this one battle — that would be enough. He will then be seen as a man of the future, a man of vision. Who will dare doubt his word again?

Liu Fang has been working toward her Master's of Arts in Cinematography at the Beijing College of Broadcasting. She has just published her first novel, "Small Fish and the Piglet."

Age 31 · **Occupation** Hospital staff physician in Chongqing · **Family** Single
Home 100 m², three-bedroom condominium · **Free time** Surfing the Internet,
playing poker, fishing, watching TV · **Monthly income (RMB)** Personal –

LI QIHUI

Doctor
Chongqing

4,000+; Household – 4,000+ · **Household budget (RMB)** Housing/Utilities
300; Education – n/a; Parent support – 0; Health care – 0; Food/Clothing/
Other – 1,000; Savings – 2,700

7:50 在手机闹铃声中醒来，总习惯再小睡一会儿。8:05 不得不强打精神起床，用冷水洗脸，激励制服肌肉的神经，才有好的状态去迎接工作中的问题。

8:30 每天的工作是从例行的交班开始，看看有什么危重病人需要特别留心。今天交班总算有好消息，医院打算团购住房，听说在江北，价格也较便宜，许多老同事都心情一样激动。

10:30 上午还好不是太忙，看了几个病人，只是一些上呼吸道感染和胃病，在留察病人中有个以前我的老病人，今天特别看看，看起来明显好转，病人家属都很感激，又加重了我喜悦心情。此后又收来3两个发冷病人，感到事况又急不错，心中想希望把交班状况作持到明天。我们值班是24小时，下午和晚上想睡觉的时候，行好哪大家同事一起游泳，也在晚上睡个好觉。

下午2:00 今天怀没想到这么忙，从12:00开始一直不停有病人来，大多是腹痛发热等，都是些在休息时间来看病，连喝水的时间呼都没有，更别说吃饭了。还好值班这天我们下午可以休息3小时，将抓空时间吃午餐饭。2:30可以去看房。

下午5:00 看房归来，不是很满意，环境不好，结构一般，卧室大小，我喜欢大的，回来时我已很疲惫，可以小睡一会，5:30好接班。

下午5:30 小想质宣真好，然而心中暗自嘀咕，今晚不会太忙吧，凭经验讲，我们这种阴沉情况下，病人总是会来很多。

下午7:00 在外喊了炒饭，刚尝来朝着病人了，北头不好，不出所料，其后就一直没歇过，大部分发烧发热的。现在是禽流感期间，每个病人都要求作胸片、上专胸科查看作详回联络予我记录。还挺着...感冒引起，要不然我也会很随离去观察。

晚8:00 刚才抽空吃了几口冷炒饭，又来病人了，这时冷室外传来孩哪那事乱那怕的脚步声，呼叫疾步的喊声，心里一紧神经绷到高度紧张，拿出看，果是来的你，找3口先交给外科，医务外理。暗想，又有外科的事了，够他忙的。

晚8:10 没想到刚们的腹腹和呕吐多又来的那，这次更严重病人，大概是急性胃病，看看我急诊不释了，主即送入抢救室，呕吐，测血压，听呼吸看瞳孔作详回查些，当病人总好些很好，先因为把急救车令评估作详正常，接着洗胃，胃中没有剂有等物质，马有密切观察病情老化，并同情服药治疗，同时支持其丈夫。细任查找我唇舌，还有无斑疹等。

晚9:00 又走病人一位，医院虽无床，但也在坚持。可能还需一段时间，从发炎者吃药可能性大，需要考虑因为丈夫原因，持向丈夫支持病人及妻属在，要尽量让她放情平稳。处理完病情后，向我朋友发个短信，祝她生日快乐。

晚9:40 又看了几个病人。又时抢救室有出来哭闹声，原来病人已身陷半身瘫痪，陪伴护车仪器，大声骂着丈夫。同情的人不一定多，细看她的疼痛等波及我们科，我们已过太多事情。现在社会经济发达了，思想开放了，但人而来更为复杂，恨也无法损及他们及社会造成多一方面过重负担呢。

凌晨1:30 与倒座来半已算睡觉了，而我还在不断的看病人。刚好来加以的发热病人，停止其在抢救室生辰，心中很高兴。多医生最大的希望是找到病人的病因解决，至少我这么认为。那前有些来的病人已经全愈，要求回家，向他们交待一些注意事项后同意出院。在临走时丈夫说着对我说声"辛苦啦"。

凌晨2:30 同又接个19岁的孩，呕血的。看有无胃肠接荡，需要与其在陪，但她及同行的人身有带作现钱是为多不够。打电话给她父母，居然她父母也没钱。让她吃点药就可以了。心中一阵气，在此如此，娘娘的孩子他们一道，才勉强同意明来拿钱来。最后只有让她先在行观察，收住院，拿药方去配，当地已欠的那

Li Qihui's Diary

7:50 – I was awakened by the alarm on my mobile phone. After struggling to get up, I washed my face with cold water to give myself a little shock and brushed my teeth.

8:30 – My work began with the regular change-of-shift briefing. In addition to finding out which patients need what special care, I got some other good news: that the hospital intends to purchase a block of apartments for employees, and that the prices would be relatively low.

12:00 – The afternoon got really busy. Patients came in one after another, most of them with stomach aches or fever.

14:00 – Fortunately, we had a three-hour break in the afternoon. I made use of the time to have a box lunch so that I could go look at the apartments at 2:30 p.m. Once I saw them, I didn't like them nor the neighborhood either. The buildings were just standard fare with small bedrooms, but I like big ones.

17:00 – I was very tired by the time I got back to the hospital. I handed over the shift and took a 30-minute nap

19:30 – I ordered fried rice from a place outside the hospital. As soon as the fried rice arrived, a patient came. As expected, I had no rest after that. Most of the patients had fevers. Everyone is worried about bird flu these days. A chest x-ray and routine blood tests were ordered for each one, and we recorded all of their contacts, just in case. Fortunately, their fevers were all caused by colds.

20:10 – A female patient was rushed in unconscious. Her condition suggested that she may have taken something in a suicide attempt. I administered some medication to keep her vital signs at normal levels. Then her stomach was pumped. I told her husband to search their home carefully for bottles of medicine.

21:00 – The patient hadn't regained consciousness, but her blood pressure was back to normal. I wondered whether marital problems had been the cause of her suicide attempt. I explained to the husband that she needed to be kept calm after she woke up.

21:30 – Cries and shouts came from the emergency room. The female patient had awakened and had yanked out her transfusion tubes. She was cursing her husband loudly. My guess had been right. We'd seen so many cases like this. As the economy has been growing, so has the rate of infidelity and divorce. Many families are unstable.

1:30 – The patients with fever had returned to normal, and the patient who had tried to commit suicide had recovered and wanted to go home.

2:30 – I examined a 19-year-old girl with abdominal pain. Suspecting she might have intestinal blockage, I ordered her to be admitted immediately. The problem was that her parents only had 1,000 yuan, and that wasn't nearly enough. Her parents told me just to prescribe some medication for her. I was very insistent about her staying, so they reluctantly agreed to bring some money the next day. The girl with abdominal pain said she had been in pain all day, but her parents hadn't wanted to take her to the hospital. It seems that the health of a daughter is not as important as money to some people.

3:30 – I was awakened by a nurse after a five-minute nap in my clothes to tend to the girl with abdominal pains.

6:20 – I was awakened again to examine patients. I felt cold when I got up.

8:30 – My shift ended at last. There was only one thought on my mind as I left: I must get to bed!

A CHAT WITH LI QIHUI

How long have you been a doctor?
About ten years. I graduated when I was 21 and got assigned to the People's Hospital in Chongqing. My specialty is cardiology, but I'm working in the emergency room right now. All of us have to work there for six-month stints because it has no permanent staff.

How do you like your job?
It's not bad. I didn't want to apply to medical school at first, but my father is a doctor and he convinced me. His point was that doctors can always get a job. I wasn't really that interested even at the beginning of medical school, but the more I learned, the more I liked it. I began to feel the sense of fulfillment in healing others.

What's your position now?
Physician-in-charge. It takes about five more years to become Associate Professor of Medicine and another five years to become Professor of Medicine, the highest level.

So you could reach the highest rung on the ladder by the time you reach 40?
Only in terms of hierarchy. There is no limit to your technical skill development. You have to keep learning. Pharmaceutical companies, both Chinese and western, sponsor seminars with experts in cardiology and that helps.

Do these companies sell instruments and equipment to your hospital?
Some do, and some don't. Foreign companies invite us to take part in all kinds of events. But domestic companies still lag far behind in terms of technology. So they resort to other methods, like bribes. Most large seminars and lectures are sponsored by foreign companies, and they take place

here almost every month. Whenever a new drug is launched, for example, we learn about its use and effects. We can't learn everything, but these meetings help a great deal.

How has the medical reform affected your work and personal life?

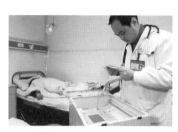

The reform changed many things. When I started in 1996, I earned less than 200 yuan a month. With the reform, Premier Zhu moved to triple doctors' incomes and raise their status to public servants. Two years later, I was earning 700 yuan. Also, our new hospital president at that time used some funds to increase our bonuses. They were raised from 50 to 300 yuan per month and now they can be as high as 2,000 or 3,000.

Is it true you have to have "guanxi" (connections) or be willing to bribe someone in order to get a good doctor to treat you?

I don't think so. Our society is more transparent now. People are more aware of their rights, and if they have a problem, they can call a hotline. The media also likes to expose scandals. There may be a few unscrupulous physicians, but most adhere to professional ethics. We used to think only about how best to heal patients. Now we also have to consider a patient's ability to pay. Many believe that doctors prescribe the most expensive drugs in order to get higher commissions. Of course, some doctors bear responsibility here, but the point is that medical treatment used to be covered by the government. Now that people have to pay their own bills, they watch every cent.

I understand you are single.

Yes. I have a new girlfriend though. She's an accountant at a bank.

Any marriage plans yet?

Marriage is not for me. I thought about it when I was younger, but I like my freedom. If I got married, I'd be accountable to someone. I don't do that much for fun – just poker and fishing – but I enjoy having time for myself. Even if I found someone who likes to do the things I do, it still wouldn't work. I've seen what has happened to so many friends.

Aren't there any happily married couples in your circle of friends?
Not really. A pretty girl I know married a rich man who sometimes strays. She doesn't lose her temper when he does, though. She just makes him pay a 5,000 yuan penalty whenever he doesn't spend the night at home. It's not that people of my generation don't want to get married. We're just a little afraid of it.

How do you think marriage today differs from when your parents were young?
People of my parents' generation have a very strong sense of responsibility. This is what kept families together.

Do you live alone?
Yes. I live in a condominium downtown, which my parents helped me buy.

And where do your parents live?
They live in housing provided by his hospital. Though my father is a retired professor, he still works – and earns a lot more than I do. Many hospitals still want him because he's an expert. Like most children of highly respected parents, I feel under pressure to succeed.

What do you do in your free time?
I watch TV, surf the Internet. On weekends, I meet with friends. I also eat out quite a lot.

It seems you live a happy life. Do you have any particular worries?
Sure. I worry that I might not be able to live the way I'd like to. I hope my career will be even more successful than my father's. I want to buy

a nice big house and a BMW. Right now I only have a compact car – it's an Elanta. Those are my two goals – very simple and pragmatic.

What do you think of your country and its development?

I'm of two minds. The standard of living is definitely improving, but manners have fallen by the wayside. People seem to have grown indifferent to each other. They used to live in harmony, to share a single yard. As for the future, the prospects are not bad in general. The government is paying more attention to

the need for social harmony and is concerned with matters like the income gap and the problems of farmers. But there are so many people in China. The education system can't accommodate everyone, and we also need a better legal system, so that laws can be enforced consistently.

What do you think about other countries?

Many have stronger economies, like Japan and Korea. Their societies seem more cohesive to me, and that's what is most lacking in China. When Korea was caught up in its financial crisis, they called on the rich to help. That would never happen in China. The rich here are less educated and cultivated. I haven't traveled beyond Hong Kong, but I have a friend in America, and I have a good impression of that society. In America, people don't rely on "guanxi" to get promotions like they do here, but on their ability. If I had the choice, I would go to America.

THE HAIRDRESSER'S TALE
by You Fan

Hongying is 36 and a hairdresser. She lives on a hill in Sichuan in a village called Xiaoyuan. Here in the hills, it is rarely as foggy as down on the Chengdu plain. Even on this fall morning, the sun can be seen peeking out over a hill, just beginning to shine into the home of Hongying and her ten-year-old daughter, Xiaocui.

Hongying has already lit the stove and dished up two bowls of heavily seasoned noodles. This is their usual breakfast fare, nothing that would cause Xiaocui's young face to flush. This morning, Xiaocui has to ask her mother for 250 yuan so she can join a hobby club. Xiaocui knows before she opens her mouth that this will set her off.

"What?" cries Hongying, "That's the fifth time this term! What's it for this time? A building fee? A test fee?"

Xiacou explains that it is for membership dues and that her teacher said that those who didn't join a club showed no ambition. All they could expect from life when they grew up, she said, was to be farm workers here in the hills.

"... and I've already said I'd join the Drawing Club," Xiaocui says.

"Don't they teach you how to draw in class?" asks Hongying.

"All we get taught there is perspective," Xiaocui says. "And we get the same lesson over and over. In the Drawing Club, we get to learn how to draw sunflowers. And I love drawing sunflowers. Please!"

Hongying sighs and gets the 250 yuan. Hongying has no husband. When Xiaocui was still a baby, he was sent to prison for three years. Every month of those three years, she took provisions to him. On his release, he came back home, but he was like a stranger. Prison had changed him so profoundly. He was not the man Hongying had married.

232

The stranger stayed a year and a half. One day, he walked out without a word. Hongying never saw or heard from him again. For the last five years, she has been managing on her own.

This morning, as soon as Xiaocui leaves for school, she hurries around, tidying up her shop. The day after tomorrow is a holiday, so she will be busy until then. Before opening the door, though, she sits down in front of the mirror to make sure she looks presentable.

Although she is no longer young, Hongying believes that as the only hairdresser in the village, she has a responsibility to keep up with hair-styling fashions. So she watches television with a particular eye to the hairstyles of popular music groups, like F4 of Taiwan, or movie stars, like Pei Yongjun of South Korea. How Mariah Carey or Sophie Marceau wear their hair does not escape her either.

Television is by no means her only source of fashion news. Over her 16 years as a hairdresser, Hongying has trained nearly 200 apprentices. Although they are all now scattered across the country, many have stayed in touch. Yesterday evening, for instance, one of them, Luo Xiaoyan, called her from Shenzhen. She was full of hairstyling news. She said that straight hair was out – no more ionic iron! – and that the marcel was back in. She said you can already see lots of marcels on the street. There appear to be two variations, she said – one is to curl only the ends of the hair, leaving the hair near the scalp straight, and the other is to curl the hair closest to the scalp and leave the ends straight. She said the second variation was to produce a more Bohemian look.

Hongying sits in front of the mirror, trying to think where Bohemia might be. She wonders, again, what her life might have been if she hadn't waited all those years for her husband. Would she have got married again? Could she have gone to somewhere like Bohemia? Too late now, she says to herself.

The Town Governor's wife is now at the door. When Hongying opens the door, she rushes in in a flurry, explaining that she is leaving the country in two days for Singapore, Malaysia, and Thailand. It will be her first time in any of those places. She says she saw a new hairstyle on television last night called something like "Mia" and wonders whether Hongying can do it.

"Bohemia?" Hongying asks.

"Yes! That's right," says the Governor's wife with delight.

Hongying nods. It will be good to try out this new type of marcel wave, she thinks. As she expertly runs her fingers through the Town Governor's wife's hair, all thoughts of her absconding husband and the Drawing Club dues slip out of her mind. She calls up the words of Luo Xiaoyan from last night. Silently practicing her pronunciation of "Bohemia," she again rises, as she always does, to the new challenge.

You Fan is a freelance writer, whose published works include "QQ's Two Fingers Zen" and "Songjiang's Happy Life." You Fan's novella, "The Accident at the Police Raid on Chunxi Road," won a Red, White, and Blue Literature Award in 2004.

Age 45 · **Occupation** Maid in Chongqing · **Family** Husband, 21-year-old daughter, 19-year-old son, father-in-law · **Home** 70 m², three-bedroom apartment · **Free time** Occasionally watching TV · **Monthly income (RMB)**

LI SULAN

Maid
Chongqing

Personal – 600; Household – 1,300 · **Household budget (RMB)** Housing/ Utilities – 200; Education – 0; Parent support – 0; Health care – 100; Food/ Clothing/Other – 800; Savings – 200

11月28日　　星期一　　阴

　　今天早晨我6点钟就起床。起床后就把我一家人早饭做起。一家人吃完饭后，我就准备上班。

　　上班的第一件事就是买菜。我走在路上心中想，今天潘老师的儿子上学去了，没在家，可以就买小菜在菜市场，买了省菜、白菜、四季豆、筒子骨炖汤就那么少。大约在8点多钟就到了潘老师家，开始一天的上班。我为潘老师一家做早饭，早饭做好后我又接着做清洁。从楼上一层一层往下做，心中想，到要仔细做干净。中午只有我和潘老师两个人，所以简单的几样菜，做个清汤，就可以了。吃完饭后我把厨房擦得干干净净的，又接着做上午没有做完的清洁。大约下午四点钟我就扫了一遍干干净净的房子，锁好了门，我就先下班了，快到家了听到我们小区的一位邻居说，我们房子又要拆迁了，以前分屋只分16.5平方米，现在要分18平方米，每人要多1.5平方米，我一想，我们家要多17.3平方米，可以抽个时间去向领导读一下，如何解决，这对我们家

6:00 – I got up and made breakfast for the family.

7:00 – The first task today was to buy groceries for Mrs. Pan's family. I work for them as a maid. On the way to the market, I remembered that Mrs. Pan's son had gone to school and would not be home, so I only needed to buy a few things today. At the market, I bought lettuce, cabbage, kidney beans, and "soup bones."

8:00 – I got to the Pans' and started work, including making breakfast for them. Then I started cleaning the house and, later, prepared lunch.

12:00 – Mrs. Pan and I ate lunch together. I had made some very simple dishes and a soup for the two of us.

13:00 – After lunch, I swept the kitchen thoroughly and went back to cleaning the rest of the house.

16:00 – After checking to see that everything was tidy, I locked the door and started home. As I neared my building, I met a neighbor who told me that our building was going to be torn down and that we were going to be resettled again. Originally, each person had been allotted 16.5 m^2 of space, but that had been raised to 18 m^2. For the five of us, that would mean another 7.5 m^2 in space. I decided I needed to talk to the authorities about this.

17:00 – Having realized that my son was supposed to work the night shift that day, I rushed home to make dinner. Sometimes, if I don't get home in time to wake him up, he oversleeps. After dinner, my son left for work, and I straightened up the apartment, watched TV (news, soap operas, documentaries) for a while, and then got ready for bed.

20:30 – I went to bed. I have to get up early, so I go to sleep early, usually before 9 p.m.

A CHAT WITH LI SULAN

How are your children doing?
My daughter is out of a job right now. She used to work at the New Century Supermarket, but I asked her to quit because it wasn't safe being out that late. She would work from 2 until 10 p.m. Once a man on a motorcycle offered to take her wherever she wanted for 2 yuan, but fortunately she didn't go with him. The main reason why she only finished junior middle school is that we couldn't afford her tuition, even though she was a very good student. Her father got very sick about the time she was preparing to take the senior middle school entrance exam. His medical expenses came to more than 10,000 yuan at that time, and that put us in a very tight spot. Our land is gone, too. It was taken from us in 1995.

How was your life when you still had your land?
Life was much better. We had a 30-year contract for the land. We planted and sold vegetables, which gave us enough income to save a little money. Now we can barely cover our living expenses. Back then, we could save 4,000 or 5,000 a year. We also had four or five pigs, which we would fatten up with red potatoes and then sell. All that went to savings because the money we earned for the vegetables was usually enough to cover the essentials. At first, we refused to sign the resettlement contract, but we were finally forced into it. If we hadn't signed, they would have thrown us in jail. Several people I know went to jail for refusing to sign. My husband's illness began after our land was expropriated. We had no land and no work, and he was very sick.

What did he have?
Asthma. After we lost our land, he went to work for a chemical plant, which produced paints and pesticides. He was hired as a porter making a little over 1,000 yuan a month. It all started with a cold. He

received very poor care, and his cough got worse and worse. Meanwhile, he was inhaling poisonous fumes, which made him sicker and sicker. In the end, we paid around 40,000 or 50,000 yuan for his treatments. That was the money we had saved over the years for our children's education, and soon it was all gone. So there was none for our daughter's tuition. I told her I'd borrow the money for it, but she refused. I was very upset at the time and cried a lot.

Where did you live after your land was taken from you?

We rented a house at first. In 1997, we got our compensation for the old house, but it wasn't much – about 10,000 for the land and the house together. On top of that, the house they built for us to move into was so poorly constructed that the property management bureau wouldn't give us a certificate. They made us stay there, though, and gave us compensation of 81 yuan a month to make up for it. Finally, they decided to settle matters once and for all and paid us 21,000 yuan last December.

How have you been making ends meet?

Before my husband got sick, I worked in the same factory wrapping pesticides. Then with his illness, I was the only one working, trying to support us and two children in school. In the meantime, I've worked in all kinds of places, even in other cities. But I worried when I was working so far from home. About nine months ago, I went to work for Mrs. Pan as a maid. Her home is near

mine, and the job is not very hard. My husband hasn't worked in seven or eight years, but my son works as an apprentice lathe operator. It's hard when you have someone sick at home. As soon as you earn a little money, it's spent right away. We can't save any more like we did when we still had our land.

What expectations do you have for your children?
It depends on how much effort they make. I hope they will be able to learn some skills and earn enough money to live reasonably well. People living in the country can't afford to be out of work for long. My daughter is still young, but it's not easy for her to find a full-time job.

What do you think about all the growth in Chongqing?
The people in the city wanted to expand, and they have taken our land to do it. Our life is worse now. There used to be 13 working farms in the area, and now there are only four. We had more flexibility when we were working our land. We would work here a few days and then a few days somewhere else. We went wherever there was work. If I couldn't work one day or got held up by something, I could work faster the next day. If I had something else to take care of, I could finish my work ahead of time. That's impossible now.

Are you interested in national events?
Yes. But like everybody else, I am mostly interested in the things that directly affect me. Like the price of natural gas. It's gone up to 80 yuan for one can. I had wanted to have it put in our apartment, but now that it's going to be torn down, they won't do it. About the rest, there's not much we can do but watch the news on TV. President Hu Jintao says the country will develop harmoniously and the farmers' problems will be solved. I watch very little TV now.

Your apartment is very nice, so modern and well furnished.
Our home is very poor compared to Mrs. Pan's house. But I was able to buy some new things for it because I ran a small restaurant downstairs before working for Mrs. Pan. I earned almost 100 yuan a week selling noodles. This lasted only a year, though, because most of my customers were construction workers, and they left when the building was finished.

Age 43 · **Occupation** Associate professor of computer science at a Chongqing university · **Family** Husband, 17-year-old daughter · **Home** 120 m², three-bedroom apartment · **Free time** Reading, entertaining, traveling, computer games, DVD movies, helping with daughter's homework · **Monthly income**

SHENG MINGYU

Associate professor of computer science
Chongqing

(RMB) Personal – 4,000; Household – 9,000 · **Household budget (RMB)**
Housing/Utilities – 3,000; Education – 2,500; Parent support – 100; Health
care – 1,500; Food/Clothing/Other – 1,400; Savings – 500

　　当熟悉的早安的音乐响起时，是早晨七点。新的一天郁源开始。

　　记得有句名言，每天的太阳都不一样。我懒洋洋地躺在床上，让先生将窗帘拉开一半。外面没有太阳。在这个城市，这个时候，太阳对人们来说，是一种奢望。不管怎么说，每天的太阳都不一样，每天的生活也不一样。

　　伸个懒腰，翻身起床，开始品味一天的生活。

　　一边洗漱，一边同先生谈论着今天各自的工作计划，脑海里却在飞快地思考着早上一、二节的课。都说电影是门遗憾的艺术，直到放映前，导演都在反思，某个细节是不是还可以做得更好。当教师又何尝不是呢。第二天要上的课，前一天就开始思考所要讲授的内容，重点是什么，难点在何处，如何组织教学，如何让学生听懂，怎样启发学生的思路，教学内容如何安排，逻辑结构是什么？如何引入所讲授的话题等等，这一系列问题会不停地在脑海里滑过。即使是这样，每次上完课，仍总觉得还可以改进，好在教师这个职业，会给你改进的机会，不是吗？等第二次上同一门课时，你会在前一次的基础上加以改进。

　　"我今天中午去看晓晓"，我一边打扮着自己，一边对先生说。"噢"。先生应答着，拿着自己的公文包。

　　先生在政府部门工作，遵守严格的作息时间──早九晚五。中饭由单位提供。先生近几年开始发体，本来也没有觉得有什么不好，但考虑到健康原因，他也

SHENG MINGYU'S DIARY

7:00 – From the radio I hear the song, "Wish you a good morning." I stretch, get up and already begin to enjoy the day. I wash and dress, discussing today's plan with my husband, then reflect about my first two classes. I drink a glass of water with a vitamin pill and warm some milk in the microwave. I dunk bread into it for breakfast. If I have no class, I usually fry an egg. I rarely have breakfast out. My husband, who works nine-to-five for a government department, will get his breakfast there.

8:00 – We leave home together. My husband says that helps strengthen the ties between married people. (Before my daughter entered senior high school, I walked her to school every morning.) It takes me five minutes to get to the classroom. Classes are usually given in a multimedia classroom, and I need time to get ready. Although I could, I never lecture sitting down. I like to face students directly and watch their expressions. Because of the microphones, a teacher can speak in a normal tone and walk around the classroom. You can establish closer contact with the students that way, and I think that makes for a more personal, relaxed atmosphere.

9:00 – During the ten-minute break between classes, I turn on a little light music for my students to help them cool down mentally. Students don't clean blackboards after class for teachers like I did when I went to school, but I told my daughter that teachers really appreciate help like that. Now she often cleans the blackboard for her teachers. I used to be proud of the respect students showed me, but I don't see much of that anymore. A lot of students think you're just doing a job they're paying you for.

10:30 – After class is finished, I go back home before going off to see my daughter at school (Note: Sheng Mingyu's daughter has leukemia). On the way back, I take care of a few things for my daughter. She asked us to buy her some books, some fruit, and a few necessities. As

I wait for the bus, I recall that my daughter used to hold my hand when she was young. I sometimes squeezed her hand for fear of losing her. She's grown now and taller than I am. Now she helps me get on the bus and holds my hand – I think to steady me.

11:30 – I arrive at my daughter's school. She hasn't gotten out of class yet, so I go into the "House beside the river," a small restaurant, and wait for her there. There are only six tables, but it's clean and nicely decorated. The restaurant is near a branch of the Yangtze River, and you can see it from the windows. I order seasonal vegetables and bean curd. The meal is ready just as my daughter arrives. While we eat, she tells me about her day. My daughter isn't a big talker, but she opens up when she's with me. I always hoped my child would be like this – a woman of few words who knows how to defend herself. I prefer to be a listener when I'm with her. I may remark about an opinion that seems extreme or immature, but I do it gently, and she tends to be reasonable. Parents of adolescents don't always have it easy, but with patience and honesty, as well as love, it can work. In fact, my daughter and I are more like friends than mother and daughter. I discuss my worries with her and she is always recommending books and movies to me. She says it helps close the generation gap and establish a shared language. In the middle of the meal, my daughter's cell phone rings. She answers with, "Donald Duck!" This is what she calls her father. He calls her Mickey Mouse. Hearing the two chatting happily makes me feel very good.

13:00 – After lunch, my daughter goes home for a short nap. Before I head back, I ask her about her eating. She says she feels tired after class and has no appetite. I remind her that she needs to take care of her health.

15:00 – After having a cup of tea at home, I sit down to read.

18:00 – I take a break and do a little cleaning. That's my job. We hire help for spring cleaning, but I do the routine housekeeping. When my husband comes home, he makes the dinner and washes the dishes. That's his job. I curl up on the sofa and read the newspaper while he's working. When he is done, we go out for a walk. We've been taking evening walks for years. Many important decisions have been made at these times. After exchanging a few words about what we've done today, the subject shifts to our daughter. My husband is always full of delight when he talks about her. We come back home after dark and make another cup of tea. Then we busy ourselves with our own things. He usually reads the paper, while I prepare for lessons. Occasionally, there's an interesting TV program we watch together. A friend once said to me: "How happy you are! Your daughter is beautiful, your husband is considerate, and you are successful in your career." As a woman, I am satisfied. I want everything, but it's better not to have it all. Zhuang-zi wrote in the Warring States Period that faster horses die earlier, sharper knives go dull sooner, and better wood is the first to be felled. I have thought about this for many years and finally realized how true it is.

A CHAT WITH SHENG MINGYU

How long have you lived here?
Five years. The apartment is provided by the university. It's 120 m², but with the closed-in patio, it is really bigger than that.

Are you originally from Chongqing?
No, I'm from the Northwest. I studied at Northwest Normal University and got transferred here in 1998 from Lanzhou. My husband is from here, but we met in Lanzhou, where he was in the army.

I went there to give a lecture, and that's how we met. We got married in 1987. After leaving the army, he went to work for the government at the Bureau of Land and Resources. He's in administration.

Have you been at this university since you came to Chongqing?
Yes. I was already an Associate Professor at Lanzhou Business School. At that time, our child was very young, and I had fewer things to worry about. Then I was often just physically tired. Life is simpler now in some ways because our child is older, but I am often mentally tired. To become a full Professor, I have to publish and do a lot of research. So I've had different tasks at different phases of my life. As an Associate Professor, I was busy with my child, and now that I have less work with my child, I am busy with becoming a full Professor. Priorities shift as life progresses. I love my career, but there is a limit to my energy.

Is this a picture of your daughter? She's very pretty.
She is – and already 1.74 meters tall. She is in her third year at Banan High School, which is a very good school. She used to come home on weekends, but now she only has half a day off every week. She has to study all the time, but that's the way it is.

How do you do that?
We don't allow her to study when she's on vacation, for one. I have

her go traveling. She's visited almost half of China by now. I think it's important that she meets new people and broadens her perspective. But I don't pressure her. She'll go to college if she passes the exam, but if she doesn't, it doesn't matter. She could go abroad instead. She says she would like to go to Britain.

Why Britain?
Because she has a close school friend there, who's told her a lot about it. Originally, I wanted to have her study at a foreign university because I don't think our system is very good. But I wonder now if it would really be safe for her to do that. She's still so young.

Would it be a hardship to pay the high tuition there?
I don't think we're completely prepared to take it on right now, but we'll do the best we can. My husband and I agree on this. We own three apartments, one of which will pay for her tuition in Britain. Our income is not that high, but I would say we're relatively well off.

It sounds like your family is doing very well.
Well ... there is one thing, though. I don't usually talk about it ... My daughter has an almost incurable disease – leukemia. They discovered

it during school break this year. Perhaps she should stop studying, but I think it would be too depressing for her to have to stay at home or live in some kind of hospital. She needs a lot of care and shouldn't get too tired or bleed. This will probably have an impact on her plans to study. She is not as physically strong as others. We are not sure how this will affect her college entrance exam. It's hard to say. Time will tell.

Your daughter must be very brave.
Yes. As painful as it is, we all have to do what we have to do. I look at my

daughter not as a patient but as a normal person. My mother had cancer, but she faced her illness with a positive attitude and eventually overcame it. My family has been through a lot of suffering and come through it all somehow. My job now is to protect my daughter and help her get well.

How have the great changes in China over the past three decades influenced your personal life? If the Cultural Revolution hadn't ended when it did, I would have had to go to the country, since I was the eldest child. My life would have been totally different. That was a terrible time. Many bright people lost the opportunity to be educated and have good careers. Life takes a different course depending on the husband you choose too.

How have the changes affected your life since you started working?
The whole opening up of China has had an impact, but reforms at the university have been particularly significant in my life, of course. Today, for example, you can no longer give your students low grades or set strict requirements. If you fail many students, they probably won't be able to get a job. So there is a kind of quota system.

Is this a problem?
A big problem. Some teachers get threatening calls from students, who say "Watch out if you fail me on the exam!" Students have changed a lot too – they want overnight success. Companies do need qualified graduates, but only 25 percent of this year's graduates have found work, I hear. Life has become very competitive.

What could the rest of the students do?
It depends on their attitude. They could start at the bottom and work their way up the ladder. Many could get jobs as civil servants or teachers and make a decent income.

What do you think about China's prospects as a society?

I don't know much about politics. I care, but I have no say in it, though I am a Communist Party member. I joined when I was a graduate student. Today, I think our national policies and overall situation are generally good and reasonable, though there have been problems in implementation. But that's a process and can't be changed overnight. Ten years ago, for example, no one could afford an apartment, but now nearly everyone can. People are hopeful about the future. If they weren't, how could they go on living?

What are your thoughts on the outside world, on other countries?

I've never been abroad, so what I know comes from the news or what I hear from others. I believe some foreign countries are more harmonious than ours (less competitive and single-minded), judging by the young visitors I've met here. They seem very different than our young people.

In what way?

They strike me as happier, better adjusted. Our students are under terrible pressure. They're nervous, and so are their teachers. In many foreign countries, people believe that a sound mind and a sound body go together, but here physical education is considered a "corrupting  influence." The young people from abroad I have met also seem to take care of each other. Older brothers and sisters take care of younger brothers and sisters. Most of our children have no brothers or sisters. I like children a lot, so I also have a strong opinion about the one-child policy. What children need is a healthy environment – not necessarily comfortable, but healthy. The policy deprives me of my rights. If it were just a recommendation, I might accept it. But considering the quality of life, I might not have had a second child anyway. Our standard of living would definitely be lower.

What else do you have strong opinions about?

The health care system. Medical costs, for one, have become almost unbearable. I once asked the doctor about an anti-inflammatory drug he had prescribed for my daughter. It seemed strange to me because they hadn't found any inflammation during the tests, and he couldn't tell me where it was. But he insisted on the drug anyway. I later learned that the price of the medication was twice its cost to the hospital. It was then clear to me why he wanted to prescribe it.

What did you do?

I asked a friend, and he said it didn't matter either way. So I had her stop taking it. She began to feel better immediately. I took her home and began to care for her myself. Nutrition is more important than treatment, I believe. And 20 days in the hospital cost us almost 20,000 yuan.

What were you able to do for her at home?

I learned on-line that she should have blood transfusions, so I donated my own blood. That's the safest and best way. You have to understand the processes involved, I think, and not just sit there and put your destiny in someone else's hands.

What are your dreams?

That my daughter is healthy and has a good life, and that no one else in my family gets sick.

THE TRAFFIC COP'S TALE
by Enya

Squeezing through the narrow urban canyons of Nanchang, the morning sun sends rays of gold out over the traffic on Bayi Boulevard. (During the Red Years (the Cultural Revolution), the powers-that-be here liked to name whatever they built "Bayi."[1] So today there is Bayi Gardens, Bayi War Memorial, Bayi Square, and Bayi Boulevard.) At precisely 8 a.m. at the busiest intersection of this boulevard, Luo tugs down the jacket of his police uniform, straightens the brim of his cap, and steps up onto the traffic dais. Luo is 28 years old and tall – 1.8 meters to be precise. Standing on the high box in the middle of the intersection, he knows that he cuts an imposing figure.

Before his appearance, drivers have been blowing their horns and cursing each other out their windows to get across the intersection. As soon as Luo mounts the dais, all traffic stops, waiting for his first signal. Luo's face, neck, and arms are darkly tanned, the handiwork of weather endured at this intersection over five years. Even at his throat, where his jacket collar doesn't quite meet, there is a small triangle of tanned skin. Looking at Luo now, at this man so self-composed and full of calm authority, it is difficult to imagine him as a small boy, let alone the mischievous small boy that he was. This is a man who has no need to ever raise his voice. Not even when he is being harangued by drivers proclaiming their innocence. So absolutely sure of himself is Luo, so confident of his authority, so very diligent that, for every one of the last five years, he has won an award of one kind or another, and has indeed been held up as a role model for all traffic cops.

His father is very proud of him. He has taped all the programs on which Luo appeared and has saved all the articles in which Luo was interviewed. He has even saved articles in which Luo only got a passing mention. Looking at the pictures of him, it's easy to see why he has so often been put forward as the archetypal policeman: His arms held authoritatively aloft, Luo has the serious look of a leader of men. When Luo was at school in the 1970s, the boys in his class were asked

1) "Bayi" means August 1st – the Founding Day of the People's Liberation Army

what they wanted to be when they grew up. Almost without exception, they had wanted to join the People's Liberation Army. Practically every one of them has ended up today in jobs not the least heroic. They are businessmen, lawyers, doctors, techies. Luo's job is also not heroic, but an aura of something akin to it seems to cling to his uniform. At 5:30 p.m., Luo steps down from his dais. Even with breaks, a day of holding up his arms to halt and beckon traffic has made him hot and sticky. Arriving at his condominium in a nice part of Nanchang, he will first take a bath. After his bath, he will eat and rest, perhaps then read or play computer games. He can drop any of these in a moment if the station calls him for an emergency. But normally, he gets no night summons, so he will go to bed at 10 p.m., precisely.

Such is Luo's daily life, where the job takes precedence over everything, even love. Yes, love. Luo's unrelenting work hours cannot accommodate the impetuousness of love – there's no leaving work early or coming in late. Neither can he take calls at work, indulge in love's interminable banter. Even if a girl could get beyond such hurdles, his need to always be on call is the final blow. More than once he has left a girl in the lurch. He did have one longtime girlfriend, though. He still misses her.

At the moment, he goes out from time to time with a grade school teacher. Their families made the introduction. Luo supposes that if nothing goes wrong, he will end up marrying her. Luo also supposes that he is satisfied with his life. But if he were asked, in the strictest of confidence, if he had any regrets, he would probably say one – to have lost that girl he had for so long. Yet she was so controlling, so domineering. Surely that wouldn't sit well over time with a self-assured, strong-minded man like Luo. But bear in mind that Luo also has a secret pleasure – driving fast. In fact, so fast that he often drives well in excess of the speed limit.

In recent years, Enya has ranked among the ten best female online writers.

Age 40 · Occupation Mini-bus driver at an automobile factory in Chongqing
Family Husband, 15-year-old daughter, mother-in-law · Home 60 m², three-
bedroom apartment Free time: Watching TV, helping with homework · Monthly

YANG LING

Mini-bus driver at factory
Chongqing

income (RMB) Personal – 1,000; Household – 2,500 · **Household budget (RMB)** Housing/Utilities – 400; Education – 1,000; Parent support – 0; Health care – 100; Food/Clothing/Other – 800; Savings – 200

11月28日 星期一 小雨转阴

　　早晨6:00起床，给女儿准备早夕。说心里话，过了两周末，还真不想这么早起床，但是没办法，又一周的生活和工作还将继续。

　　6:30唤醒女儿，洗漱，整理书包，吃完早夕后，送女儿乘公交车去学校，看着女儿那幼小的身躯无奈在车里挤来挤去，心里很不是滋味，但为了锻炼她，还是狠下心来，让她乘公交车，返回家中，打开电视收看新闻节目，并与老公漫漫一起吃早夕。

　　7:40出门到车位上班，将车辆打扫干净，坐到人一上车就感觉很舒爽，这使我感到很愉快，今天车位外出办事儿不多，只出了几趟车，因为考虑经济成本，所以利用空隙时间把自己的车擦车门修好了。

　　17:30下班回家，完成每天性的清扫房间家务，无外出活动，静坐下来，考虑到近阶时间单位要进行改制，40岁以上人还要面临再就业，心里感到很茫然，做什么事都提不起精神来。

　　17:30开车去学校接女儿，利用等女儿下晚自习的时间，顺便锻炼一下身体，身体好比什么都重要，一想到女儿近期学习成绩有些下滑，心里又有些毛，说实话，我为女儿付出得比较多，但我又没想过要她长大成人后要回报我们什么，因为我不愿把它当这样沉重的包袱，我只希望她也出人头地，过上好日子，我给她的观点是，前别人是靠不住的，只能靠自己，努力学习才能改变自己。

　　21:00回到家中，安排好女儿的学习，跟他学完后让她"重点复习"，没多久，两个眼皮打起架来，很困，想睡觉。

6:00 – I began making breakfast for my daughter. I didn't feel like getting up so early after the weekend, but life goes on.

6:30 – I woke my daughter and told her to wash her face, brush her teeth, and pack her school bag. After breakfast, I walked her to the bus stop. I felt very uncomfortable as I watched my little girl squeeze her way into the bus. But that's what she wants, so I let her have her way. I went back home, turned on the TV to watch the news and had breakfast with my husband and mother-in-law.

7:40 – I arrived at work and started cleaning my bus. I drive workers around the factory sites and in and out of the city. People like it when the bus is fresh and clean, and that pleases me. There weren't many passengers today, and I made only a few trips.

17:30 – When I got home from work, I cleaned myself and did a few other chores. I sat down to think by myself for a few minutes. My work unit, the transportation department, is scheduled for restructuring soon. I'll be out of work, and that frightens me. I'll have to look for another job at age 40. I find it impossible to concentrate on anything else right now.

19:30 – I drove to school to pick up my daughter and take her to her evening study session. I did some exercising during her study because good health is the most important thing in the world. My daughter's grades have been slipping a little lately, and that worries me. I feel I've done a lot for her, and I'm not looking for anything in return. I just want her to be successful and have a happy life. I've tried to teach her that you can't depend on anyone but yourself and that you have to be independent and study hard to better your chances in life.

21:00 – Back at home, I helped my daughter get her things in order for school the next day. Then I scanned the news in "Chongqing Business." It was not long before I grew tired and went to bed.

A CHAT WITH YANG LING

How long have you been living here?
This apartment was assigned to my father-in-law in 1979 by his work unit, and my husband grew up here with his six brothers and sisters. One brother died of gas poisoning while taking a bath when he was 39. We have a superstition that something important happens to a man at 39, and that was his fate. He went out one day to buy a few things, but he didn't have enough money. As he was leaving, he said, "I'll pay for everything, dead or alive." Such an unlucky thing to say! Shortly afterward, a neighbor told him his fortune on the spot: "Somebody in your family is going to disappear." He went back to take a bath, and that was the end.

That is very sad ... Who lives here now?
The three of us live here with my mother-in-law, who is now the owner.

Do you plan to buy a new apartment?
What's the use of planning? The monthly payments would be at least 1,000 yuan, which is more than my take-home pay. If we were production workers, we probably would be able to afford it, but I'm a bus driver, and my husband is a quality assurance officer.

What are your husband's chances for promotion?
Not good. My husband got a college degree in Business Administration after working a couple of years, but he is already 43. If

you're under 35, you're a candidate for the talent bank and can be trained for middle management. People like us have only three chances: you're very talented, you're related to the boss, or you have good "guanxi."

Have you ever tried to establish "guanxi"?

My sister's husband drives for the top boss, but he doesn't like to take advantage of this. But my sister wanted a better position and badgered him every day until he talked to the boss about it. She now makes a little more, about 1,000 a month.

Does your factory have any plans to improve benefits?

The company is going to offer company cars soon. As a worker, you buy the car and then get reimbursed for 35,000 over three years. But people like us will never get that because we can't afford to keep a car. It costs 10,000 a year to maintain it, and you can't sell it for five years. So, for us, that money is just a mirage.

How about social benefits?

We do have retirement benefits, a housing fund, and medical and unemployment insurance, all according to the amount of your salary. We've been paying for pension benefits right along, so we're not worried about retirement. If I pay in 200, the company adds 600.

I understand your daughter is in a very good middle school and doing well.

Yes, she is in her third year now, 15 years old. We paid 30,000 – which we had saved up long ago – to get her in this school, and we may have to pay several thousand next year for high school. So there's no point even talking about buying a house.

How is the outlook for your job?

I am at a crossroads. With the new company car program, many people will buy their own cars, so I will be out of job as a driver. I could probably only become a porter or a janitor.

What are you going to do?

My husband suggested I retire and get a one-time package. That would be worth 40,000, but I would still have to pay pension and medical insurance for a long time, so I would run out at some point. If there is nothing else for me, I could start a housekeeping business. But my big dream is to run a home for the elderly. Couples in the cities often have two children and also parents to take care of, but little time. So there is a need.

Good idea. What does your daughter think of your idea?

My daughter doesn't like the idea of a housekeeping business, and me working like a maid. Her schoolmates are not as poor as we are, but I tell her not to compete with them. Everyone is unique. I want her to live a better life, but we basically don't have the means. We will only be able to afford an average, not a great university. There are jobs these days for barely half the college graduates, so where you go really counts.

What do you want her to be?

I hope she will be a doctor or a teacher. She wants to be a doctor because she thinks teaching is too exhausting. She thinks it is noble to heal others.

What do you think about your country and how it's developing?

Comrade Deng Xiaoping used to encourage a small number of people to get rich, and now, in the 11th Five-Year Plan, everyone is being encouraged to get rich. I think this is good. Life is much better now than before. But my mother-in-law always praises Chairman Mao. Her family used to be very poor, but now things are much better.

Do you see any areas for improvement?

Yes, health care and education. Our textbooks told us that capitalism was inferior because people couldn't afford health care. But it's just the opposite. Capitalist countries provide health care support, while here you need to have a lot of money in the bank in order to go to the  hospital. Also, about half of the family income goes for education, and poor families simply cannot afford the high tuition. I think medical and education costs should be adjusted to people's income. China is leaping forward, but we still earn very little. We are too large to fit the mold of other countries, and our culture is so different. Mazda workers in Japan earn terrific salaries, I hear, but what about us? Something needs to change.

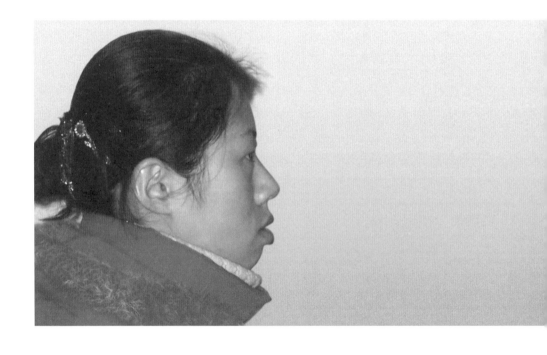

Age 25 · Occupation Middle school teacher in rural Chongqing · Family
Single, living with parents · Home 70 m², three-bedroom apartment · Free time
Watching TV, shopping with friends · Monthly income (RMB) Personal – 900;

Wu Shuang

Middle school teacher
Rural Chongqing

Household – n/a · **Household budget (RMB)** Housing/Utilities – paid by parents; Education – n/a; Parent support – 300; Health care – n/a; Food/Clothing/Other – 600; Savings – n/a

吴爽 女 25岁 共青团员 毕业学校 渝西学院 工作 4年
日记时间：2005年11月25日

　　我是一名热爱教育事业的人，也是一位热爱学生的人，或许是受了家庭环境的熏陶和影响，爸爸妈妈一直都希望我能在长大以后走正路，堂堂正正做人，踏踏实实干事，经过数十年的寒窗苦读，终于在2001年从位于重庆永川的渝西学院毕业，又十分幸运地到了北碚区晏阳初中学任教，所教学科是英语，成为了一名光荣的人民教师，我的心情在上班之初是非常阳光而且抱负远大的，我认为我会让我的人生理想在我的工作中得以提高，实现以及升华，因为我既是一个开朗活泼的女孩，爱说爱笑又爱动，而且我还是一个很理性很明辨事理的人，所以我在工作中很受领导的赞许和学生的喜爱，而且我感到非常的幸福。由于我家距离学校较远，而且我有时要上早自习，所以我就有住在学校的时间，但即便如此，我爸爸也会从家里带给我来自家庭的幸福和温暖，以及我最爱吃的食物和小点心，真的让我好开心，一方面这是来自家庭的关爱另一方面就是因为学校的伙食质量实在让人不敢恭维。

　　今天又是在学校住的，所以早上睡到七点四十五分才起床，以最快的速度刷牙，洗脸，擦乳液，然后梳头，连眉毛都没划，最后穿上鞋有冲办公室。最近忙起来的时候都这样，所以也已经习惯了，冲了两袋豆奶，吃了几块饼干，边吃边浏览一下今天上课的内容。下早自习了，大约八点十五分，科代表抱作业来了，又有五、六个人没交作业，但我点儿都不生气，习惯了。只是让科代表叫同学一定要在规定时限内做完交来。喝完豆奶，把盅盅洗了，上课预备铃响了，我拿了课本和备课本，粉笔，快步走进教室，还挺安静的，师生相互问好，我说：Class begins! 学生一边起立一边齐说：Stand up! 我又说：Good morning, class! 学生又说：Good morning, Miss Wu. 然后我说：Sit down, please. 学生齐说：Thanks you, Miss Wu. 之后坐下就开始上课。首先复习了一下昨天的内容，我问全班一齐答：What do you do? I'm a student. 纠正了student的读音后，我抽学生单独一个一个地来问答，其中有一、两个仍然不会说，我有点恼火，严厉地批评了他们，并且让他们一直说正确为止。然后进行新课 What does he/she do? 先由 What do you do? 引入，让学生自己领会 What does she do? 的意思，并作导他们作答。在作答的过程中，教授了新单词：worker, farmer, driver, etc. 大约抽了四五个成绩较好的学生与我操练。然后全班操练，同时板书，较熟悉后同桌操练。下课铃响了

Wu Shuang's Diary

7:00 – Last night I stayed overnight on campus because my home is quite far away and I sometimes have to be at school for morning study sessions, like today. Getting up a little late, I quickly brushed my teeth, washed my face, slapped on some lotion, dressed, combed my hair, and rushed to the teachers' room for breakfast. There I drank soybean milk I mixed from a powder and ate a couple of biscuits. All the while I was looking through the material for today's class. (I teach English to third-graders.) A little later, the English Subject Representative (a good student in the subject) came in with the homework books. I saw that five or six students hadn't handed in their homework again, but this happens too often for me to get upset about it anymore.

8:00 – After the bell rang for the first period, I did our usual ritual: I say (in English), "Class begins! Stand up, please!" All 50 students stand up, and then I say, "Good morning, Class!" and the students answer, "Good morning, Miss Wu." Then, I say, "Sit down, please." The students answer, "Thank you, Miss Wu," and sit down. We began with review. I asked the class, "What do you do?" The class answered in chorus, "I'm a student." One or two were still not getting it right, so I told them they had to repeat the answers until they did. I went on to the new lesson – grammar. I chose four or five good students to practice a conversation with me in front of the room, and then the whole class practiced together. The bell rang signaling the end of the first period.

9:00 – I drank water during the break. When the bell rang again, I spot-checked pairs of students as they conversed in the classroom.

10:00 – I didn't have a class for the third period, so I spent most of the time reading the preparation materials on English and Political Science for my exam. I have applied to study education at the Southwest University. I think I'm strong enough in Political Science, my field of specialization, so I normally spend more time on English. I spent the last few minutes preparing for the fourth period.

11:00 – The children were a bit loud when I entered the room at the bell. I waited for them to settle down and then announced the start of class, just like I had done earlier with my other group. I reviewed the material from the day before and worked with them on grammar, but the class was getting more and more unruly as I went along. Finally, I had to stop ten minutes early to spend some time reestablishing order.

13:10 – By the time I got back to my dorm after lunch, all my roommates had already fallen asleep. I lay down and slept.

15:20 – I woke up and tidied my bed and belongings. Then I went to the fourth floor of the school for a Political Studies meeting to discuss the latest government policies. These meetings are reasonably organized, but sometimes there's not as much content as I would like. They also sometimes run overtime. You don't want to fall asleep, though. You lose face completely if you have to be wakened. After the meeting, I waited a while for the school bus to take me home.

18:00 – I finally arrived home. I had dinner with my parents and watched TV. Afterwards, I went to my room and read for a while. During these last hours of the day, I like to read relaxing and entertaining books like Qiong Yao's romance novels and magazines like Elle so I can fall asleep easily later. I got a phone call from a friend of mine. After chatting for about half an hour, I washed up and started to feel a little sleepy. There was nothing interesting on TV.

23:20 – I turned off the lights and went to sleep.

A CHAT WITH WU SHUANG

How long have you worked at this school?
Three years. I graduated from college in 2002 and came here directly afterwards. I am one of ten English teachers, and each of us has about 100 students divided into two classes. Most of our children come from rural areas, and only a few will probably pass the senior middle school entrance exam.

How do you like being a teacher?
I think I have matured a lot since I started. We have much to deal with here because the children aren't used to sitting and listening. They haven't been brought up with a lot of discipline in this sense. It's especially bad in English class because they see no value in it. Children in Shanghai probably do see the value, but our children don't expect to ever speak to foreigners or travel abroad.

Have you ever been promoted?
The first year was a trial period, so I was officially appointed in my second year as a Level III middle school teacher. I was promoted to Level II last year, since I had earned my Bachelor's degree from a correspondence school. When I first came here, my salary was about 500 yuan, with a bonus of 100. With the promotion, I now earn 600, with a bonus of 300. Teachers at better schools earn money by giving lessons on the side. But none of our children here want extra tutoring. They don't even take regular classes seriously.

Does that meet your needs?
I'm unable to save anything right now, though my parents might be able to save some of the money I give them each month. Though my mother is retired, my father works at the same school I do.

Did you want to be a teacher when you first graduated from college?

I went to a teachers college, so I definitely knew I wanted to teach. But it was hard to find a job at first. At the time, schools didn't need a lot of new teachers. You had to have great "guanxi" to get a decent position. I got this job through the Education Committee, which assigned jobs to students. Later on, when there were even more applicants, graduates had to look for themselves. My job is not bad. Some of my classmates work much farther away from home and in even more remote areas.

What are your career plans for the future?

I hope to get a Master's in education. The entrance exam is very difficult, though, and there's a lot of competition from recent graduates who haven't been able to find a job.

Your school is named after Dr. Yan Yangchu: In 1943, he was known as one of the ten great men who had made the most revolutionary contributions, along with Einstein. He claimed there was no student who could not be developed. Do you believe that?

Well, here in the country, it's very hard to accomplish that with students because they are so strongly influenced by their family, which generally has no formal education at all. So, you can improve the facilities and increase teachers' skills, but most children tend not to see and take advantage of these opportunities. Maybe it would help if we teachers had more incentives. There is such a big difference between salaries in the country and the city. Teachers there work hard too, of course, but they don't have to waste their time constantly disciplining students.

Do you have much time for entertainment?

Entertainment is for weekends only. I'm exhausted on work days.

I usually study for the entrance exam after work, and I'm also taking a preparation course for it. So that doesn't leave me much free time. On weekends, I often go to the city and meet with my old classmates. I don't have a boyfriend, though. People are always putting pressure on me for that because they think I'm getting old.

What do you like to read?
I don't read much, I'm afraid. I think it has something to do with the environment here. I don't read newspapers or magazines. I do watch TV, but only pure entertainment and occasionally a movie.

What do you think about the many changes China has been undergoing?
Tremendous changes have taken place, of course. Most young people today haven't had to endure hardships the way my grandfather and grandmother did. Things are progressing reasonably, but there's still a  lot missing, including in education. For one, I feel it is overly exam-oriented. It should be more quality-oriented. Also, creativity is generally not encouraged. University enrollment has gone up in recent years, and most students who pass the entrance exam eventually get into a university. But there is another side to the coin. A lot of graduates have problems finding jobs. I'm planning to get my Master's, but there is no assurance I'll get a good job afterwards.

Is money for graduate school a concern?
Yes. If I quit my job to study, it will be very expensive. I'll have to rely on my parents again. Since I've been working, they've been able to relax a little. But they are very supportive of my plan – and I will look after them later, of course.

What do you think about foreign countries?
In terms of education, they seem to have good systems. Here, we have nine years of compulsory education, but it's not applied consistently. Education in other countries seems more open and democratic, and their students more creative. Here they seem only good at taking exams. Chinese students may win awards in the Mathematics Olympics, but foreign students will perform better in practice, I believe.

Do you have negative impressions about any foreign countries?
My impression of the U.S. certainly isn't very good. I just see too many reports on terrorism and political hegemony. But I don't really know much about the American people.

If you could choose to teach in any country you wanted, which would you choose?
I would go to any country that attaches great importance to education. As for daily life, I would like to live in France. I think life there would be very interesting.

The Coal Miner's Tale
by Liu Tong

Is time asymmetrical? We wonder that out here in West China. Especially when the mail seems to go around and around in circles before it gets to us. But it eventually does get to us, most of the time. On this very day, for instance, by way of waking me, Sister Cai pushes a crumpled envelope under my pillow, making it even more crumpled. I don't complain. I know that Sister Cai will let me have time before work to read it. Which is why sometimes it is so much better to have a woman as your boss: A woman knows that it's not just a matter of reading what is on the pages. She knows you need time and space in your mind to call up and re-experience the relationship with the writer of the letter.

In the next room I hear the shift changing over. Some of the workers are taking a shower. Others just wash the coal dust off their faces. They may look fit for public display, but the smell of their sweat remains. Pity the rest of us.

The letter — only a month old according to the postmark — is from Cong. We were at middle school together. Then Cong was adopted by his uncle and moved away. Now he is studying at a university in Changsha. He writes that he is worried about me. At school, Cong and I were inseparable. We had our own secret place to meet, which required climbing up on a wall and edging along the top, legs dangling, until we were out of sight. We used to sit there for hours on end, talking about a favorite poem, like the Changhen Ge, or reciting back and forth the Weiyangqu.

In his letter, Cong says that he has read on the Internet that miners in West China are paid only 1 yuan for each bucket of coal; that they can barely afford to eat; and that there are fatal accidents almost every day. He promises me that as soon as he graduates and starts his own business he will send for me. I smile to myself, touched by his concern. It makes me feel warm and good inside, like I feel when I look down at a bowl of hot soup sprinkled with freshly chopped spring onions. I also smile to myself because his concern is misplaced. In my mind I begin to phrase a reply to his letter:

"My dear Cong,
Our life here is nowhere as miserable or boring as you have been led to believe. There are plenty of jobs here other than working at the coal face ..."

One of those jobs is to allocate equipment and supplies, like lamps and work clothes. The boss, I'm sure of it, thinks that because I went through senior middle school I am more adaptable than others. So I get moved around from post to post. And these changes keep me interested in the work. Nor is the work itself that arduous. I earn 1,300 yuan a month, which is also not bad. The one thing I do miss, and I must tell Cong, is having someone like him to share a dish of braised pork with. Of course, on my present wage, I could easily afford a dish of braised pork. But such a special dish has to be eaten with the right person — and there is no one here like that. Yes, I must tell him that. That's not to say that we don't enjoy ourselves here. Sometimes, when we have a holiday, we get all cleaned up — even those stinkers who usually only wash their faces — put on our best clothes and go to town for a drink or two. We feel, at last, that we're truly living, not just working and sleeping.

By this time, I am now dressed and have placed Cong's letter on the bed. Lying down on my stomach, I start writing my reply. Sister Cai puts her head around the door just then and barks: "No time for that! Get to work!" Throughout the day, as I go about my work, I think of past conversations with Cong and of more things I want to tell him. I will tell Cong that, no matter what the season is, down here it's always black. For color, we have satellite TV.

Sometimes, after I come off shift and shower, I watch "Super Girls" with the others. This program gives us more to talk about than anything else. We argue over who is the prettiest, the best singer, everything and anything. You won't believe how passionate the arguments are, how wrapped up in these girls we become – girls not one of us will ever meet! Even my little brother is obsessed with these Super Girls. In his last letter to me, he enclosed some pictures of one of them, Li Yuchun. This pleased me inordinately, if only because it is by such small tokens that we realize how much we are loved.

It also served to reassure me once again that I had made the right decision. As I will tell Cong in my letter, I must stay here two more years. Each month I can save 1,000 yuan and continue to support my little brother until he finishes school. What, though, if Cong's worries are justified? What if there is an accident in the mine? Even if I am not one of those injured, I will still have to look elsewhere for a job. And I may never find another boss as understanding as Sister Cai ...

My roommate has just finished his nine-hour shift and gotten ready for bed. Pen in hand, I decide I won't tell Cong of my fears. Why worry him even more? My roommate asks from his bed if he can see my pictures of Li Yuchun. If I let him, he says, he will ask his young sister to send him pictures of some other Super Girls. Now that's something to look forward to. Especially, as I now have it on good authority, time actually is asymmetrical, even here in West China.

Liu Tong is a television producer and writer from Hunan. He is the author of the novel "The Deep Blue of Fifty Meters," among other published works.

Age 15 · **Occupation** Middle school student in Chongqing · **Family** Parents
Home School dorm, moving to apartment near school · **Free time** Reading
short stories and magazines, listening to music, surfing the Internet · **Monthly**

CHEN YUEYANG

Middle school student
Chongqing

income (RMB) Personal – 0; Household – 8,000 · **Household budget (RMB)** Housing/Utilities – 1,000; Education – 4,000+; Parent support – 0; Health care – n/a; Food/Clothing/Other – 1,000; Savings – 2,000

12月 1日　周四

　　早上灯亮的时候起动。居然根本不知道。而学校又很夸张的用广播放歌。开始还好，很小声地放钢琴版的《我看歌声的翅膀》。后来突然用可以杀人的声量放了一首迈克尔·杰克逊的歌。可怕啊——不过如果没有这首歌我估计我们寝室也醒不了。

　　生活老师太神奇了，一个一个门敲过来看都没看就在"咚咚咚"地敲门后说了一句"还有两个!"回走一看，果然，只有两个人爬起来了，对面的两位仁兄还在睡觉。

　　结果害我洗了脸了姜雨婷才缓缓起来，她说其实她二十分钟前就醒了。但一直没起来是在做心理斗争。很痛苦地斗争了二十分钟。

　　而孙丹是绝对的心理素质好，一般来讲我

跟李萧萧（？）梳头，擦脸后她才起来，而且表示没有听（？）放歌与生活老师敲门。

　　出去后买早饭。方舒曼说他们学校早上六点多就开始大声放歌被亭边的居民告了。但李萧萧习惯性的翻白眼，说："这个星期放的歌实际上更加炸爆了！"然后跑去买了一个粽子。

　　今天买粽子的人出奇多。从人里重挤了很久才挤到一个卖相奇惨的粽子。结果李萧萧那个完全没有卖相#@！？……

　　到了教室想起了今天彭老师叫我收语文作业。飞速在黑板上写"语文作业　快做！"写完就马上听到身后一齐发出的"哇——"然后大约一半的人到处找人借来抄，一半的人自己飞速做，就是用那种每道题不超过五个字的写法做。比如瞄一眼类似于"为什么原句某某某中用'体

CHEN YUEYANG'S DIARY

6:20 – The lights went on in the dorm, and music began playing over the PA system. The first piece wasn't so bad – a piano version of "With the Wings of Songs," which was played very softly. But then, all of a sudden, a Michael Jackson song began blasting out of the speaker. Horrible! But many of the girls in my room would never wake up without that volume. This whole piped-in music idea is crazy. I washed and then went to eat breakfast

7:30 – Arriving at the classroom, I remembered that Mr. Peng had told me to collect the literature homework for today. I wrote on the blackboard: Literature homework. Do it now! After that, I heard some yelps, and more than half the class started racing around looking for homework to copy. What a world! I had done mine, of course, but at the cost of not doing my Physics homework. In our room, Sun Dan got up at 4 a.m. and finished all the homework, and there were eight or nine others in our grade who had managed to complete everything too. I saw some of them with steaming coffee on their desks. Recharging their batteries, I suppose.

8:30 – The second class was History. Mr. Yang, a substitute, had us recite from the book on our own. I heard students in Group Four reciting from the Industrial Revolution chapter, while I was working on the French Revolution. I started to have a stomachache, which got so bad that I finally had to ask for permission to go to the bathroom. By the time I got back, class was over.

12:00 – After cleaning our room during the noon break, I worked on a paper for Mathematics. (I was so glad my extra hour of English had been cancelled for the day!) I worked on it until 2 p.m., but finished only half of it. I packed my bag and rushed to the next class.

15:30 – When it was time for Gym class, Li Yuke said we could go downstairs and play without teacher supervision. No one would be allowed to stay in the classroom. I was torn. I had so much homework to do. Just then, Wang Jiangxue called out to me, "Come on! Let's go play badminton!" So I tossed down my pen and ran downstairs after her. Gym class is intended to make you exercise, but these days that's considered almost degenerate. Gym class is now for reading course material.

17:00 – I ran to the cafeteria and bought some hot and sour noodles to keep going. I hurried back to the classroom to eat and do some homework before Physics started at 5:30 p.m. The subject was buoyancy, which my teacher had said was easy. All we needed to do was to analyze the forces and use the formula to calculate it. As I looked over the questions about chain wheels, levers, atmospheric pressure, and buoyancy, the left side of my head began to ache.

18:30 – Classes for the day were finally over. I hurried back to our room with piles of homework, hoping to be the first one in the shower. But Jiang Yuting and Sun Dan beat me again, and I had to wait until the lights went out to shower. While my hair was drying, I got my books out to do homework. Today was such a full day. Except for Literature and Math, I was given a huge load of homework in every subject. I also have to do a lot of reading for History and Politics. Monthly exams are coming soon.

24:00 – But this is it. I'm not doing anymore homework tonight. It's time to sleep. I hope I can. Sun Dan will be up in just four hours. Good night.

(This diary was written right before Chen Yueyang moved into an apartment close to the school with her mother.)

A CHAT WITH CHEN YUEYANG

How do you feel about the upcoming high school entrance exam?
This year has been very intense. I feel under a lot of pressure. When we entered the third year, we were divided into groups on the basis of our grades. That means that everyone in my group is also a good student, which puts us under even more pressure. If I don't do well on the exam, I will lose face. We have tests every month now, and a performance ranking for the class is posted after every test.

What's your ranking right now?
It's between 40th and 60th. There are over 600 students in my grade, so my ranking isn't too bad. But we will be competing with thousands of students from other schools, too, and the good high schools have very high admission standards. In the end, probably about a third of us will get admitted to a high school. You have to take a lot of classes there, including lab courses if your grades are good enough. For those courses, you can't buy admission, so it's terribly competitive.

How much would it cost if you have to pay to get admitted?
Around 30,000 yuan. You usually pay about 100 yuan for every point below the minimum entrance score.

How long do you study every day?
I usually study in the morning before class, between classes when I can, and then after dinner until 11 or 12 p.m. – about six hours a day. During finals, it's more of course. Some students in my dorm sleep only an hour or two a night. They study until 1:30 a.m., take a short nap and they're back at work at 3 a.m. It's horrible!

Of all the subjects you take, which ones interest you?
There are several I really like and think will help me in the future. One

is Math. I also like learning English vocabulary, especially terms in Biology and Geography, which should be very useful later. Writing from memory in Chinese is also interesting. But there is a lot that seems so unimportant, like Contemporary Chinese Literature.

With such a strenuous schedule and little exercise, do students often get sick?
I don't know of anyone who has gotten sick so far this year. We all exercise with jump-ropes after the second class each day. And we eat better than we used to. I'm taking vitamins and calcium tablets to help stay well – and also because I want to be taller. Some of my classmates are taking pills of various kinds, whatever the ads say are good for students during exam time.

What do you do with your friends when you have time?
We do homework together and go out to get something to eat after school. But we don't usually have time for sitting around and just talking or playing games. Sometimes we get in touch during holidays, but the most time we spend together is during lunch break and dinner.

What is popular among students right now?
Music, for one. Zhou Jielun is very popular, and so are Avril Lavigne, West Life, and Blue. About a third of the class, I would say, listens to Japanese and Korean singers, like Dong Bang Shin Ki, WINDS, and Kang Ta. I like Ayumi Hamasaki and singers from Hong Kong and Taiwan, like Liu Dehua and Zhou Jielun.

How do you usually spend your weekends?
We have only Saturdays free. There's school on Sunday too. I sleep on Saturday, usually until noon, because I really need it. And then I do

schoolwork in the afternoon. How I spend the evening depends on how much is left to do. If there is a lot, then I have to study. I'm comparatively lazy, though. While I'm wasting time sleeping on Saturday morning, other students are taking two hours of extra classes.

Are you taking any extra classes?

I take an extra class at school at 5:30 p.m. four days a week: Mathematics on Monday, English on Tuesday, Physics on Wednesday,  and Chemistry on Thursday. We have to pay for the extra classes, but they're not expensive. One class costs only 40 yuan, since it's held at the school. Outside classes cost more. I'm taking an extra English class, for example. I go to my teacher's home most days at noon and every Friday afternoon. This class is more expensive – 50 yuan an hour, which amounts to 300 every week.

What do you think about your teachers?

They're serious in class, but can be quite funny after class. Some chat and play basketball with us. Young teachers will talk about pop stars with us, and sometimes we have heart-to-heart talks with some of the older teachers. I talk with my teachers whenever I am having trouble with something. My favorite is Ms. Chen. She teaches Math, but she also knows a lot about advanced technology. She talks to us about how to become an integrated person, one with self-confidence and humility at the same time. Last year, she even played basketball with us from time to time.

Do you know what you want to do in terms of career?

I want to be a doctor working with Doctors Without Borders. They don't earn money for their work. They're volunteers on missions to help people in countries in crisis.

How will you earn money then?

I plan to work for six months each year to earn money, then spend the next six months doing volunteer work.

Why do you want to be that kind of doctor?

I've wanted to be a doctor for a long time. And after I saw a program on television about Doctors Without Borders helping victims of terrorist attacks, I knew right away that that was something for me.

Where do you want to study?

Australia. I don't want to take the entrance exams here. I'd rather go abroad. I'm so tired just preparing for the high school entrance exam, and there will be far more pressure at the university level. There are only 24 hours in a day, and that won't change to 36 just because we're preparing for an exam. Someone once said to me, "Don't think the third year in middle school is the Eighteenth Level of Hell – that's reserved for students taking  the university entrance exam!" Besides, I think I can get a better education abroad. I doubt that I'll be admitted to a very good university if I stay in China, and the alternatives are worse than the universities abroad. The environment is better there too. I like clean places.

Age 69 · **Occupation** Retired professor of preschool education in Chongqing **Family** Husband, two grown children, one grandson · **Home** 80 m², three-bedroom apartment · **Free time** Watching TV, listening to music · **Monthly**

DENG DAI

Retired professor of preschool education
Chongqing

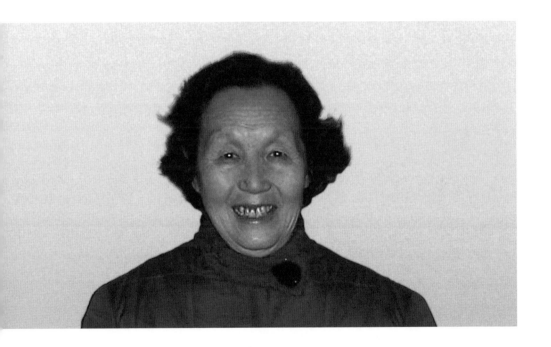

income (RMB) Personal – 1,500; Household – 4,000 · **Household budget (RMB)** Housing/Utilities – 500; Education – 0; Parent support – 0; Health care 1,000; Food/Clothing/Other – 1,000; Savings – 1,500

一天的生活日记

我是一个高校退休教师，在解放后的中国生活了五十六年，现在感到生活一年比一年幸福，真可谓是"英雄开花节节高"。虽是我已年近古稀，却深感"夕阳无限好，只是近黄昏"，但我仍然要"把握住这晚年的幸福，让生活过得更有滋味。

我对幸福的这种感觉是来自我的切身体会。首先，现在我不会再天提心吊胆，怕搞政治运动，别人再斗我。（因文革中，我在一个中学国家在此海外关系教师，被强加为升学主义，经历了批斗、游街、批斗、劳改的全过程）政策现在人不敢斗那现在我参加了民主党派中国致公党，受到应有的尊重，我感到心情舒畅。二是不再为经济上的拮据而节衣缩食，国家上恋着了，我现在可随心可做了。（工作四十年工资仅为57元，我与爱人收入共为120元。安养住的五口之家好容易真是提示艰难时，现在我们二人每月收入赚一毛钱却要考虑是怎该用近4000元，就我们二人消费，我已觉十分宽裕了）三是，人际关系简单了，退休了也不必再因为升普级问恼，与同事们发生矛盾，与同事之间的关系自然也就和谐了。

退休了，有了属于自己的闲暇时间，该如何度过，我是一个很普通的人，没什么抱负，只是要把珍惜这一生剩余的时间过得轻松一些些，愉快些输快些，我没啥别是任何的招样，就是平静地过完每一天。

我一天的生活大致是这样度过的：每天早上约7点半-8点起床，梳洗后作简单的早餐，牛奶、馒头或自火卷面包，或牛奶冲芝麻粉超市买的（豆浆、黑豆、芝麻、核桃粉……）因我的肠胃不好，吃不下太多的食物。早上还吃一粒合施尔康（含各种维生素、微量元素）。上午外出买菜、购物，有时专挑附近菜场买些小菜来回折多小时。有时则上街购买肉食、蔬菜、水果，需1-2小时甚至3小时。提回数斤重的食品货到回来。我当然是时候锻炼身体，但每次买菜就是一次体力的锻炼。午餐，吃得较简单，面条、蔬菜、鸡蛋，馄饨、饺子、烧饭（炒或蒸各种蔬菜）午餐约11.50看快的饮食。午餐时看电视中央台的新闻与香港凤凰台的节目，时事辩论会，有快的误中午，还天午12睡2小时，冬天有时睡1-2小时，有时不睡。下午看的报纸、杂志、串门，与同事们的电话聊天，内容是互通信息如校内外有关情息，尤其与自身利益有关的情息，如退休职工女如果你外好，医疗费怎样用更合适，哪个商场菜的菜种食品价廉物美。（以商场黑木耳、白糖、减价、牛奶降价……主不要买打农药的叶子蔬菜（喷了保鲜剂）），交流作菜的经验会如粉面苗排骨怎么做

页　章

DENG DAI'S DIARY

About me, I'm a retired university professor and have lived in liberated China for more than 56 years. My life is becoming happier and happier. Although I'm almost 70 years old, I sincerely feel very happy as I approach the autumn of my life. My feeling of contentment comes from my own personal experience. I no longer live in fear and trembling. I needn't be afraid of political upheavals nor worry that someone might bring trumped-up charges against me. I experienced the humiliating process – searches, seizures, denunciations and rehabilitation through forced labor during the Cultural Revolution. Today, I'm a member of a democratic party, the China Zhigong Party, which is one of the eight "democratic parties" that provide consultative advisory services to the Communist Party. I'm respected both politically and personally. Plus I no longer have to live on a shoestring. Our combined monthly income is almost 4,000 yuan, which I think is just plenty for the two of us.

7:45 – I got out of bed, washed up and combed my hair. I had milk with steamed bread for breakfast, though sometimes I make a nutritious mixture of soybean, black bean, sesame, and walnut powder in milk. I have some trouble with my digestion, so I have to watch what I eat.

9:00 – I took my multivitamin and left for the market. Sometimes I buy our food at the market nearby, and then I'm finished in half an hour. But today I decided to shop farther away, which can take up to three hours in all. In the shops, I bought several kilos of fruit, vegetables, and meat and then walked home. I don't get much regular physical exercise, so shopping and having to carry a load is actually good for me.

12:30 – I made a simple lunch – noodles, vegetables, eggs, dumplings, and fried rice with eggs and vegetables. If I'm back in time from shopping, I enjoy watching "Cooking Everyday" on TV. Today I missed that, but watched CCTV News and "Debate on Current Issues" on the Hong Kong Phoenix channel while I ate lunch.

14:00 – I lay down after lunch for my nap. When I got up, I considered what I wanted to do – read a newspaper or a magazine, go out to visit friends, or maybe talk with one of my former colleagues on the phone. We like to keep each other up to date on what's going on at the university and elsewhere. We're especially eager for news about our benefits. We discuss, for example, how we can make the most of our medical insurance. But we also talk about where we can buy the best food at the lowest prices or how we can reduce our electricity bill. We like to talk about cooking and remind each other not to buy leafy vegetables because they have been sprayed with pesticides.

17:15 – I started making dinner. I usually make one or two dishes of meat or fish, plus two vegetable dishes, rice, and a soup. My husband drinks a little cup of home-brewed medicinal liquor. I'm responsible for buying the food and doing the cooking, and he is responsible for washing the dishes and straightening the kitchen.

19:00 – After dinner, I watched CCTV News again, keeping my ears open, as always, for anything on the subject of government policy. There are also interesting programs on the economic channel and the entertainment channel. The latter has some good series that I like to watch about ordinary Chinese people, like "Our Parents," and "The Power of Love," as well as historical dramas, like the "The Hanwu Emperor." I also like to watch British and American movies and sometimes Korean TV dramas. I love listening to music too. Schubert's Lieder and Strauss' waltzes are among my favorites. I also like to listen to Chinese folk songs and Zhou Xuan's songs from the 1930s and 40s.

22:30 – It has gotten late, though, and I go to bed.

A CHAT WITH DENG DAI

Where did you grow up and go to school?
I grew up in Sichuan and went to Beijing to study when I was 15. My father had studied there and also my uncle, who became a doctor and emigrated to America. I went to Beijing with a classmate whose family happened to be moving there.

How did you meet your husband?
We met at Beijing Normal University. My major was preschool education, and his was fine arts. See all the paintings on the wall? They're all his. We got married in my last year in 1957 and after graduation, I was assigned to Changli County in Hebei out in the country. This was because my family was accused of being capitalist and having ties to the Taiwan Kuomintang. My husband, Mr. Wu, stayed in Beijing. But eventually the whole family, including by then our two children and my mother-in-law, were forced to come to where I was.

How was life there for your family?
The locals were not comfortable with us city people. And shortly after we arrived, the Cultural Revolution broke out. Mr. Wu's circumstances were not so good, but at least they couldn't denounce him. He had performed quite well in Beijing and also wasn't a big talker like me. I couldn't seem to keep my mouth shut. You could say things in Beijing that you couldn't in Hebei.

How did people treat you then?
Well, it started with they way I dressed. They didn't like it. When I would wear a skirt, they would tell me to wear a pair of trousers under it. And I was the only woman in town with a perm, which also caused resentment, I think. Worse, though, was having one uncle a high-ranking official in the Kuomintang and another one in America. I was treated very harshly. They hung up big signs denouncing me, searched

300

my house, and confiscated my belongings. I was very stupid sometimes too. Once, when I was ordered to hand over my eccentric clothes, I told them they were my mother-in-law's, so they confiscated her belongings too. She was also denounced and forced to sweep streets. She lived in a state of fear after that.

How old were your children then when the Cultural Revolution began?
My daughter was three and my son eight. My daughter was teased at school and frequently came home full of bruises from being pinched. In the end, the Red Guards imprisoned me, cut my hair in the half-bald style, paraded me through the streets, proclaimed me a "demon", and finally sentenced me to rehabilitation through hard labor.

Where were you sent?
To my own school. Denounced as a "demon," I did heavy manual labor, like cleaning toilets and feeding pigs. I also worked in the fields. All the "demons" came from similar family and educational backgrounds. Mr. Wu was a little better off. He was only a "half-demon." He looked after me and saw me through. The Cultural Revolution went on for ten years, basically from my 30th to my 40th birthday – what should have been the prime of my life.

Yet you seem to have remained so optimistic.
Well, I survived.

How was life after the Cultural Revolution?
By 1978, having relatives abroad suddenly became something positive, and my uncle in America was planning a visit. So I took advantage of the situation and wrote to the State Department, mentioning my uncle's visit and asking to be transferred to another school. Shortly afterward, I was able to get a job for my husband and me here in Chongqing.

So you've been living here since 1979?
Yes. When we got here, we found ourselves in a good situation, both politically and professionally. There were some problems at the social level, but that had nothing to do with the system. The system was and is very good.

Are you a member of the Communist Party?
No, the China Zhigong Party. I joined in 1983. I encouraged Mr. Wu to join the Communist Party, however, and he did. So together we formed a party alliance within the family.

What do you do at the China Zhigong Party?
We've established an office here and are involved in a lot of things. I joined the Party primarily to get to know people and make friends, since I was new. I honestly didn't expect the Party to achieve much, but many of today's government leaders belong to it – something I could never have imagined back then. Our advice is taken seriously. I'm happy that I seem to be respected again.

How would you assess your career as you look back?
I think I was lucky. I was just a regular faculty member when I first came, but later was appointed director of a United Nations project. I also had the honor of making an official visit to Japan in 1989. For two weeks, we toured kindergartens and girls' colleges that had preschool education programs. I had wanted to let one of the retired professors go instead, since they had devoted their entire lives to their work. But they insisted I go.

When did you retire?
In 1996, when I turned 60.

Have you adjusted to retired life?
I wasn't that high on the career ladder when I retired, so I didn't feel a

real loss. Retired life is very relaxing, and I need that. The first three decades of life were stressful, and the decade of labor exhausted me totally. I haven't done a thing since I retired, and my health has improved. When I first came here I was still in my 40s, and people thought I was 60! I had been badly mistreated, and the harsh climate of the north did its work too.

Now you don't look your age at all.
Since retirement, life has gotten better and better. I do what I want, and I have no regrets. And anyway, what's done is done. You can't change it.

What do you think about the medical insurance coverage you have now?
The university's medical policy is satisfactory – not the best, but certainly not the worst. Fortunately, we have no health problems right now, but

I'm saving so we'll be prepared. Some people buy an apartment, but ours is large enough, and there's no reason to make an investment like that. That money will come in handy if we get sick. The retirement benefits are also adequate. You can save some each month since the cost of living is not that high. We stay at home most of the time anyway, so we don't spend much.

How are your children doing?
My daughter teaches painting at Dalian University. She paints in the traditional Chinese style and also does something like design. She is divorced and lives alone.

And your son?
He is now in Chengdu. I worry about him because he never learned any real skills and therefore hasn't got a very good job. He was eight when the Cultural Revolution began and had to go to the country before

 he finished high school. At that time, we didn't dare dream of college for our children. Later, after the college entrance exam had been reintroduced, he tried to pass it, but unfortunately failed twice – the second time just by a little bit! He did go to night school later to study physics, but eventually dropped out and went to work for one of my cousins in his restaurant. His first wife was very ambitious and ended up going to America with their son to work. He didn't go along because he was afraid he would be treated like a second- or third-class citizen. He is remarried now, and his wife is good and capable.

BUILDING A HARMONIOUS SOCIETY
by Deng Weizhi

Historical Perspective

The recent emphasis by the Chinese government on the establishment of a "harmonious society" finds its origins in a proposal presented in 2004 at the Fourth Plenary Session of the 16th Central Committee of the Communist Party of China (CPC). This is a new development in the CPC's concept of a uniquely Chinese form of socialism, and a clear sign that its three-pronged modernization strategy based upon a socialist market economy, democracy, and culture has now added a fourth element.

The concept is not entirely a new one: efforts to achieve political and social harmony in China can be traced back over several thousand years. The concept of harmony played a role in early theories of Confucius. Confucius held that honorable people can live in harmony despite their differences. And in the fourth century B.C., Mencius (the greatest Confucian thinker after Confucius, best known for his view that human nature is inherently good) argued that mankind and heaven should coexist in harmony.

In 2002, the Chinese central government advanced the idea of coordination between the economy and society. Today, the government is advocating a harmonious society, not only as a desired state per se, but as a standard by which to compare itself to other societies.

A harmonious society and a prosperous one are closely related. Prosperity has been associated in the past in China primarily with economic development. However, an economy that is not in harmony with society surely cannot bode well for the future.

As with prosperity, a harmonious society and a stable one are closely related. Without social stability, there can be no harmony. Once stability has been achieved, a society is then in a position to advance to greater harmony. A harmonious society is thus one that exists at a higher level of social stability.

Requirements for Harmony

A harmonious society should, at a minimum, have the following four characteristics:

1. *Co-existence of different social resources.* Nationality, religion, political parties, and social strata are all important elements that must co-exist within a society. History has taught us that whenever different religions coexist and different parties cooperate with each other, there is social harmony. The national government should be devoted first and foremost to making people economically prosperous, which does not mean simply making a part of the population wealthy. A harmonious society should offer a certain degree of material prosperity to all sectors of the population.

2. *A sound social structure.* This means a structure built on balanced, stable relationships among different sub-systems, whether they are founded upon nationality, occupation, region, or family. As the framework for society, a sound social structure is a prerequisite for social harmony. A weak structure creates social distance and inequality among people, ultimately producing social tension and conflict. In contrast, a sound social structure minimizes social disparities. Within such a structure, it is easier to achieve effective social management, integration, and control – and thus harmony – at a relatively low cost.

3. *Properly managed human behavior.* As the Chinese saying goes, "you can't make a good square without a ruler, or a circle without a compass." Similarly, little can be accomplished without rules and regulations. Rules are standards of social behavior that apply to every

member of society. In theory, when there are rules, there will be order. It's like a train, which must have rails in order to move forward. Even magnetic suspension trains need rails, despite the lack of visible contact. Societal rules may be written or unwritten. Written rules include laws, regulations, codes of conduct, and certain moral dictates; unwritten rules include customs, habits, and other tacit moral precepts. Written and compulsory rules are effective, to be sure. But one does not become a person of high integrity simply by obeying the law. Unwritten, noncompulsory rules govern people's conduct through incentives and sanctions, and thus tend to be internalized. Religious beliefs also influence people's behavior and reinforce other societal controls. Social rules and norms are instruments of social control and make up the supporting framework for social development.

4. Smoothly functioning social management. Social management relates to social integration (for example, people from different backrounds working or playing together), which enables a society to effectively balance the interests of different social groups. A society which owns a sound social structure and rules but which lacks coordination among elements of society cannot achieve harmony and may result in a waste of social resources. Social structure is a framework built by people; similarly, social rules are the product of the human mind. A society that employs effective social management balances the different interests of various social sectors and promotes the optimal use of social resources.

Social Discord

Social discord has become an urgent problem in China, and the greatest source of it is the existence of two distinct social systems — urban and rural — within one society. Whether a person belongs to one system or the other depends on his or her registered permanent residence status. With this distinction come countless other dualities, whether in employment, welfare and social security, education and public services, or other aspects of daily life. This is an inequality that affects a person's whole identity. In the 1950s, the central government promulgated a series of policies and laws designed to separate the urban from the rural population in terms of migration options, food and energy supply, employment, and social welfare. The permanent residence system, in particular, seriously restricted the migration of the rural population to urban areas.

With the beginning of the reform movement in 1979, the government enacted policies to allow farmers to enter the cities and work in the construction, trade, and services sectors. It also now permits some state-owned enterprises in cities to employ a limited number of temporary and contract workers. Other types of enterprises and private businesses are also allowed to employ workers from rural areas. Aided by this policy, the rural population has acquired relatively more freedom of movement.

Has this migration accelerated the breakdown of China's dual society? Not significantly, despite a good start. China's reform in the early years began in the rural areas, and the gap between urban and rural incomes was quickly narrowed. Since the 1990s, however, growth in farmers' incomes have gone from bad to worse. In 1996, growth in average per capita income in rural areas reached 9 percent, but then fell rapidly to 4.6 percent in 1997, and reached as low as 2.1 percent in 2000. Since 2001, the central government has taken measures to reverse this trend with positive results: average incomes rose by 4.2 percent in 2001, 4.8 percent in 2002, and 4.3 percent in 2003. Unfortunately, rural incomes have not kept pace with a more quickly rising cost of living, exacerbating an already difficult situation.

As a result, the income gap between urban and rural areas has continued to widen: Urban incomes were roughly 2.6 times higher than rural incomes in 1978, improving to a factor of 1.8 by 1984; rising back to 2.9 in 1994, reaching a new high of 3.2 in 2003, and hitting a plateau of 3.2 in 2005. Considering that urban residents receive government subsidies in cash, while rural residents are subsidized in kind, the real gap is actually five to six times larger than it appears. Such a staggering gap is cause for serious concern.

China faces problems wherever the two parts of the dual structure co-exist. Since it has not abolished the system of registered permanent residence, it continues to govern the lives of all residents, from birth to death. Second, although the central government has enacted policies that enable farmers to work in nonagricultural sectors, they do not have the same job opportunities as urban residents. Their employment is hindered not only by problems such as lack of skills, but by their limited social capital as well. Because of the prejudice and distrust the system has spawned over time, farmers have a hard time accumulating social capital – such as social or business networks – and thus have difficulty integrating into the urban population. They are left with the only social capital they have – the support of fellow townspeople or relatives – to help them survive in the city. As a result, the rural-urban duality lives on within the city, where each group nurtures its own, exclusive network.

Disharmony also prevails when it comes to China's widely diverse regions. Between 1980 and 2003, the economic disparity between the eastern regions and those of central and western China widened dramatically:

· The share of national GDP of the eastern regions rose from 50 to nearly 60 percent, while the share of national GDP of the central and western regions declined accordingly.

· Per capita GDP in the eastern regions rose from 1.9 to 2.6 times that of the western regions, and from 1.5 to 2.0 times that of the central regions.

· Per capita GDP in the eastern region rose from a level of 34 to 53 percent above the national average, while that of the central regions dropped from 20 to 25 percent below the national average, and that of the western regions from 30 to 39 percent below the national average.

Despite much public discussion on the topic of globalization, we have yet to achieve the prerequisite unification that is needed within our own country. Without greater economic equality between the provinces, such discussions seem premature and threaten to widen even further our internal differences.

Another source of discord is disparity between the economy and society, more specifically between economic growth and:

· *Investment in social programs.* Our investments in science, education, culture, health, sports, and safety lag far behind those of other countries. This may not be surprising when one considers that the value of output generated by the arts and cultural institutions in America was $900 billion in 2004, while in China it was barely more than $12 billion. Spending on education by the central government accounted for just over 2 percent of GDP in 2004 – less than that spent (as measured in similar terms) by India or Turkey, and just half of that spent by the Philippines. Illiteracy is on the rise, and the school dropout rate is increasing. China's health care system ranks 144th among the 191 member countries of the World Health Organization, lower than even Indonesia or Bangladesh. China's per capita spending on health care amounts to less than half of that of the poorest country in Africa. In the past, over 90 percent of farmers had medical insurance. Today, more than 90 percent of farmers have no coverage at all. Farmers must fear illness most of all: as the saying in China goes, "ten sick people means ten poor families."[1]

· *Income distribution.* That growth in wealth should be distributed fairly within society is a basic prerequisite for social stability and harmony. There is in fact a linear relationship between the two. Since the 1980s, the Gini coefficient has been used to measure the gap between rich and poor – the higher the number, the greater the inequality. In China, the Gini coefficient rose from approximately 0.34 in 1988 to 0.42 in 2000 – certainly in the wrong direction. In China, this coefficient today is not only above the world average, but almost twice as high as that of Sweden. In the words of Deng Xiaoping: "Unfair distribution will lead to polarization."[2]

· *Employment.* Normally, economic growth leads to a higher rate of employment, since the economy is at least partially the product of human labor. Unfortunately, China's recent economic growth has not only failed to decrease unemployment, it has actually increased it. Some 200 million people in rural areas are out of work – a number equivalent to two-thirds of the entire U.S. population.

· *Human development.* People are the most valuable resource in the world. They should have the opportunity to develop to the fullest extent possible – psychologically, physically, morally, and culturally. Yet in many places in China, far greater importance is attached to material possessions – even pets are sometimes valued more than people. Statistics released by the Ministry of Health in 1998 indicate that 5 percent of the population were suffering from mental illness. For the past five years, on average 280,000 people commit suicide each year in China and each year, tens of thousands of people are killed in accidents. The rate of violent crime is consistently high. In 2003, over 18,500 cases of corruption and bribery were recorded, 123 of which involved tens of millions of yuan. In the same year, nearly 800 judges

1) Wang Weiguang, "Studies of the Scientific View of Development," Chinese Communist Party Central Committee Party School, 2004.
2) "A Chronicle of Deng Xiaoping" (Vol. 2), Chinese Communist Party Central Committee Literature Research Office, p. 362, 1993.

were punished for corruption or bribery. During the first six months of 2004, the number of public order cases dealt with by public law enforcement agencies across the country reached nearly 3 million; a 1.6 percent increase over the previous year. The number of people sentenced to death is high, and the child mortality rate, especially due to accidents, is higher than in many other countries. Are our children really the "little emperors" we say they are? This is a problem that deserves serious analysis.

The desire to solve problems is where we must begin in our efforts to build a harmonious society, and this means changing our ideas.

The harmonious society the Communist Party of China is striving to build will be unique to Chinese socialism. Steeped in Marxist thought, it will be vital and robust, growing as important social developments – mobility, equality, and others – progressively unfold. It will be a society where people and human rights are held to be central. Conflicts will arise, as they always will, but these will only shape an even richer harmony. A harmonious society cannot be built overnight. While the work has begun, much more lies ahead.

Born in 1938, Deng Weizhi is a sociologist and professor at the School of Sociology, Shanghai University. He is also a member of the Standing Committee of the National People's Political Consultative Conference. The author of over 20 books and more than 100 articles and academic papers, Professor Deng has been one of the key thought leaders supporting Hu Jintao's efforts to promote the development of a "harmonious society." He was among the earliest to conduct research on the topic, and has continued to lead the refinement of the Party's concept of social harmony. Professor Deng is the recipient of several national book awards, and has served as guest lecturer at several universities in Europe and North America, including Princeton University and Columbia University.

CHINESE POLITICAL REFORM: FROM IDEALS TO INSTITUTIONS
by Cao Peilin

Major recent political and economic reform in China began in 1978 with the Third Plenary Session of the 11th Central Committee of the Communist Party of China (CPC). While economic reform followed a step-wise progression from a planned commodity economy to a socialist market economy, political reform has taken a more erratic course, primarily due to internal and external political turmoil.

However, broadly speaking, recent political reform in China has occurred in three phases: "preparation and exploration" from 1978 to 1984; "planning and implementation" from 1984 through the late 1980s; and "assessment and re-adjustment" in the 1990s.

During each phase of political reform, the objectives have been different. Initially, reform focused on addressing the systematic abuses of the Cultural Revolution. According to the reformers, it was the excessive centralization of power, particularly at the highest levels, that proved to be the root cause of political decay during that period.

Over time, the emphasis shifted to actively advancing political reform and promoting the development of the socialist legal system. Concerns about excessive centralization of state power, and ensuring the separation of Party and government roles, were replaced by a new focus on promoting the principles of multiparty cooperation, democratic decision-making, and grassroots democracy.

In 1997, the 15th Central Committee put political reform back on the agenda again, and the 16th Central Committee explicitly appealed for the reform of the socialist system. It called for Party leadership to be involved in the development of a socialistic political entity in which the people would be empowered to rule, and the government would operate according to the rule of law. This marked the beginning of a more disciplined approach to the design and implementation of political reform.

While the early years of political reform in China revolved largely around the need for greater democracy, the focus later moved on to building the specific institutions required to support reform. Deng Xiaoping was the first of China's leaders to recognize the importance of moving from ideals to institutions when he warned that history may be repeated if "the existing system is not rigorously reformed and cleansed of abuses."

So how should China move from the ideals of reform to the institutions of reform?

In Chinese culture, society as a whole tends even now to be viewed as one big family held together by real or imagined blood relationships. Beyond its social and ethical functions, the Chinese family plays an even more important political function. The moral and ethical principles of the family have always been inseparable from politics, as the family is the basic structure upon which the Chinese state is founded. No clear distinction is made between society and the state.

The relationship between the family and the state have influenced national politics in two ways: strengthening the state's grip over the individual; while failing to protect the individual by counter-balancing the centralization of power of an authoritarian state.

We are now undergoing a great transformation in China, moving toward democratization and the rule of law under the leadership of the Communist Party. In order to build a socialist democratic system, we must heed Deng Xiaoping's warning never to ignore the pernicious influence of clan politics. It is essential that we establish grassroots organizations – cities, villages, and towns with local autonomy and authority – to replace the family as the basic unit of government. "Family and state" must be replaced with "city and state."

Born in 1933, Cao Peilin has been a professor of political science for over 50 years. Currently a faculty member of Fudan University in Shanghai, Professor Cao specializes in comparative politics, political reform, and legislative politics, and formerly headed the International Politics Department there. He counts several renowned political scientists and policy-makers in China, the U.S. and Europe among his students.

IV. APPENDIXES

OCCUPATION TYPES IN CHINA'S RURAL-URBAN AREAS

	Coastal	Inland
Blue Collar (Urban)	· Taxi driver · Waitress · Factory worker · Salesman · Massage girl · Construction worker	· Truck driver · Store keeper · Gas station worker · Railway conductor
White Collar (Urban)	· Professor · Doctor · Writer/Artist · MNC executive	· Police officer · Head of small SOE · Lawyer
Suburb	· Construction site worker (villa)	· Industrial development zone clerk
Rural town	· Township enterprise worker · Hairdresser	· Three-wheel cart driver · Hawker · Tractor mechanic
Rural	· Cash crop farmer (flowers, fruit)	· Rice farmer

Source: Mckinsey China Consumer Center

	WORKFORCE	NONWORKFORCE	
West			

WORKFORCE	NONWORKFORCE	
· Coal mine worker · Food market vendor · Bank teller · Homemaker	· Retired · SOE redundant worker · High school student	Blue Collar
· Small city mayor · High school teacher	· College student · Overseas returnee	White Collar
· Farmer in suburb · Rural migrant housewife		Suburb
· Clinic health care worker	· Landless farmer	Rural town
· Shepherd	· Landless farmer · Teenager	Rural

Urban

Rural-Urban Divide and Social Security – Facts and Figures

LARGE VARIATION IN WEALTH

USD 2005

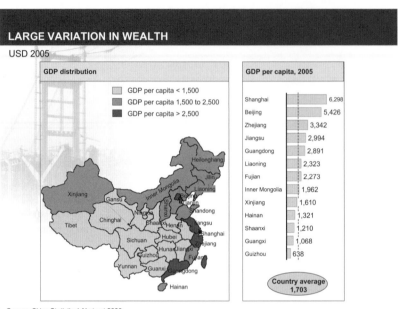

GDP distribution

- GDP per capita < 1,500
- GDP per capita 1,500 to 2,500
- GDP per capita > 2,500

GDP per capita, 2005

Shanghai	6,298
Beijing	5,426
Zhejiang	3,342
Jiangsu	2,994
Guangdong	2,891
Liaoning	2,323
Fujian	2,273
Inner Mongolia	1,962
Xinjiang	1,610
Hainan	1,321
Shaanxi	1,210
Guangxi	1,068
Guizhou	638

Country average 1,703

Source: China Statistical Abstract 2006

INCREASING RURAL AND URBAN INCOME DISPARITIES

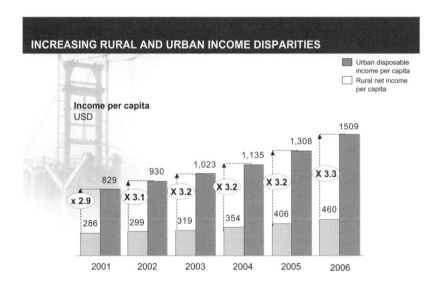

- Urban disposable income per capita
- Rural net income per capita

Income per capita
USD

Year	Urban	Rural	Ratio
2001	829	286	x 2.9
2002	930	299	X 3.1
2003	1,023	319	X 3.2
2004	1,135	354	X 3.2
2005	1,308	406	X 3.2
2006	1509	460	X 3.3

Source: China Statistic Year Book 2006

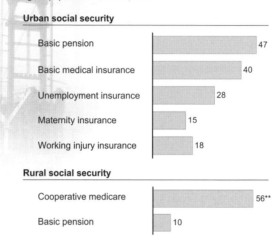

LACK OF SOCIAL SECURITY

Percent of eligible population* covered, 2006

Urban social security

Basic pension	47
Basic medical insurance	40
Unemployment insurance	28
Maternity insurance	15
Working injury insurance	18

Rural social security

Cooperative medicare	56**
Basic pension	10

* Includes working population, retirees and the unemployed, excludes children (aged less than 18) and students
** Available funds per covered life are only about 50 RMB per year; less than 20% of average rural healthcare spend per year (300 RMB)
Source: Ministry of Labor and Social Security, Ministry of Health, McKinsey analysis

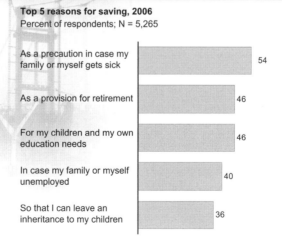

PRECAUTIONARY SAVING MOTIVE IS ALSO STRONG IN CHINA

Top 5 reasons for saving, 2006
Percent of respondents; N = 5,265

As a precaution in case my family or myself gets sick	54
As a provision for retirement	46
For my children and my own education needs	46
In case my family or myself unemployed	40
So that I can leave an inheritance to my children	36

Source: McKinsey China Consumer Center, December 2006

POPULAR TV SHOWS

TOP 10 TV DRAMA BY NUMBER OF CHANNELS PLAYED*, 2005

Rank	Show title	Number of channels played
1	"Out of Blue River" 走出蓝水岸	39
2	"Farewell Vancouver" 别了温哥华	36
3	"Dealer" 坐庄	36
4	"Heavenly Dragon" 天龙八部	34
5	"As Always" 海棠依归	33
6	"Never Replaceable" 天下无双	32
7	"Big Family" 大宅门	30
8	"Ordinary Emperor" 布衣天子	30
9	"Emperor's Son" 皇太子秘史	30
10	"Better Not Married" 不嫁则以	30

* In Chinese media, the number of channels that have purchased drama reflects the relative popularity of TV drama

**Average viewership based on total households in China

Viewership** Percent		Type	Production
	3.28	20th century	Local
	2.56	Romance	Local
	2.86	Stock	Local
	5.11	Historic	Local
	3.02	Romance	Local
	4.50	Historic	Local
	3.04	20th century	Local
	4.37	Historic	Local
	3.15	Historic	Local
	2.02	Romance	Local

Source: CSM

POPULAR MAGAZINES

TOP 10 ADVERTISEMENT-BASED MAGAZINES, 2005

Rank	Magazine title	Advertising revenue* USD millions
1	Cosmopolitan 时尚伊人	41.5
2	Elle 世界时装之苑	35.5
3	Rayli Beauty 瑞丽服饰美容	22.3
4	Rayli Women 瑞丽伊人风尚	21.2
5	Bazaar 时尚芭莎	18.5
6	Fortune 财富	15.6
7	Marie Claire 嘉人	13.0
8	Esquire 时尚先生	11.8
9	Caijing 财经	11.6
10	Trends Health 时尚健康	10.5

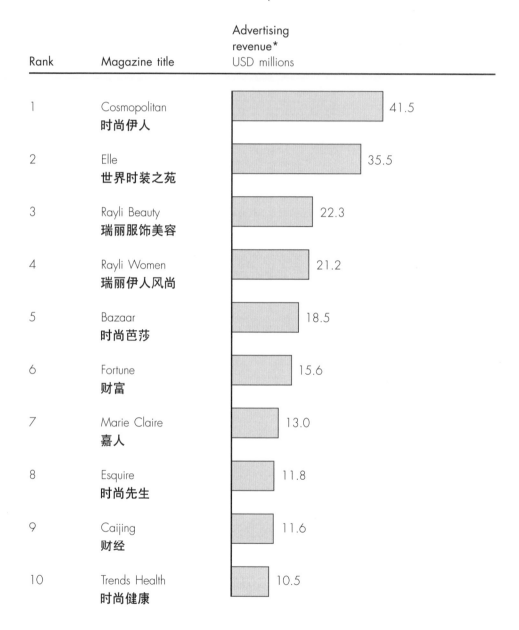

* Annualized gross figures from January to August 2005; net figures are about 30-40% of the gross figures based on a discount rate of 60-70%

Segment	Foreign partner	Local partner
Women/Fashion	Hearst	Trends Magazines
Women/Fashion	Hachette	Shanghai Translation Publishing House
Women/Fashion	Shufunotomo	Rayli
Women/Fashion	Shufunotomo	Rayli
Women/Fashion	Hearst	Trends Magazines
Business	Time Warner	CCI
Women/Fashion	Hachette	Shanghai Translation Publishing House
Men	Hearst	Trends Magazines
Business	N/A	Stock Exchange Executive Council
Women/Fashion	N/A	Trends Magazines

Source: 2005 HC Internationals

A PERSONAL BIBLIOGRAPHY

History

Iris Chang, *The Rape of Nanking: The Forgotten Holocaust of World War II*, London: Penguin Books, 1999

Confucius, D.C. Lau, *The Analects (Lun Yu)*, New York: Penguin Classics, 1990

Arthur Cotterell, *China: a History*, London: Pimlico, 1995

Stella Dong, *Shanghai: The Rise and Fall of a Decadent City 1842-1949*, New York: HarperCollins, 2001

L. Carrington Goodrich, *A Short History of the Chinese People*, New York: Harper & Row, 1943

*Ray Huang, *1587 – A Year of No Significance*, New Haven: Yale University Press, 1982

*Ray Huang, *China: a Macro History*, 2nd ed, Armonk: M.E. Sharpe, 1996

Charles O. Hucker, *China's Imperial Past: An Introduction to Chinese History and Culture*, new edition, Stanford: Stanford University Press, 1997

Keith Laidler, *The Last Empress: the She-Dragon of China*, Chichester: Wiley, 2003

Lee Siow Mong, *Spectrum of Chinese Culture*, Petaling Jaya: Pelanduk Publications, 1995

Richard Phillips, *China Since 1911*, London: Palgrave Macmillan, 1996

J.A.G. Roberts, *A Concise History of China*, Cambridge: Harvard University Press, 1999

*Michael Schoenhals, *China's Cultural Revolution, 1966-1969: Not a Dinner Party*, Armonk: M.E. Sharpe, 1996

R. Keith Schoppa, *Revolution and its Past: Identities and Change in Modern Chinese History*, Upper Saddle River: Prentice Hall, 2006

*Jonathan D. Spence, *The Search for Modern China*, New York: W.W. Norton, 1999

Ross Terrill, *Mao: a Biography*, Stanford: Stanford University Press, 1999

Social Context

Annping Chin, *Four Sisters of Hofei: a History*, New York: Scribner, 2002

James Farrer, *Opening Up: Youth Sex Culture and Market Reforms in Shanghai*, Chicago: University of Chicago Press, 2002

Vanessa L. Fong, *Only Hope: Coming of Age under China's One-Child Policy*, Stanford: Stanford University Press, 2004

Merle Goldman, *From Comrade to Citizen: the Struggle for Political Rights in China*, Cambridge: Harvard University Press, 2005

Susan Greenhalgh and Edwin A. Winckler, *Governing China's Population: From Leninist to Neoliberal Biopolitics*, Stanford: Stanford University Press, 2005

Harry Harding, *China's Second Revolution: Reform After Mao*, Washington: Brookings Institution, 1987

Peter Hays Gries, ed., *China's New Nationalism: Pride, Politics and Diplomacy*, Berkeley: University of California Press, 2005

Ma Yan, *The Diary of Ma Yan – the Struggles and Hopes of a Chinese School Girl*, New York: HarperCollins, 2005

Anchee Min, *Becoming Madame Mao*, Boston: Houghton Mifflin, 2000

*Rana Mitter, *A Bitter Revolution: China's Struggle with the Modern World*, Oxford: Oxford University Press, 2004

Simon Myers, *Adrift in China*, Chichester: Summersdale, 2002

*John Pomfret, *Chinese Lessons: Five Classmates and the Story of New China*, New York: Henry Holt, 2006

*Paul S. Ropp and Timothy Hugh Barrett, *Heritage of China: Contemporary Perspectives on Chinese Civilization*, Berkeley: University of California Press, 1990

Shi Tianjin, *Political Participation in Beijing*, Cambridge: Harvard University Press, 1997

*Arthur H Smith, *Chinese Characteristics*, Haddonfield: Ross & Perry, 2002, first published in 1894

Tang Wenfang, *Public Opinion and Political Change in China*, Stanford: Stanford University Press, 2005

Jonathan Unger, *The Transformation of Rural China*, Armonk: M.E. Sharpe, 2002

Wang Hui, and Theodore Huters, ed., *China's New Order: Society, Politics and Economy in Transition*, Cambridge: Harvard University Press, 2003

Zhou Xuegang, *The State and Life Chances in Urban China*, New York: Cambridge University Press, 2004

Economic Perspectives

Tim Clissold, *Mr China*, London: Constable and Robinson, 2004

Immanuel C.Y. Hsu, *The Rise of Modern China*, New York: Oxford University Press, 2004

Nicholas D. Kristol and Sheryl Wudunn, *China Wakes: the Struggle for the Soul of a Rising Power*, New York: Times Books, 1994

*James Kynge, *China Shakes the World*, London: Weidenfeld & Nicolson, 2006

Rachel Murphy, *How Migrant Labor is Changing Rural China*, Cambridge: Cambridge University Press, 2002

Clyde Prestowitz, *Three Billion New Capitalists: the Great Shift of Wealth and Power to the East*, New York: Basic Books, 2005

Oded Shenkar, *The Chinese Century: The Rising Chinese Economy and Its Impact on the Global Economy, the Balance of Power and Your Job*, Upper Saddle River: Wharton School Publishing, 2004

Kellee S. Tsai, *Back Alley Banking: Private Enterprises in China*, Ithaca: Cornell University Press, 2002

Carl Walter, G. Fraser, J.T. Howie, *Privatizing China: the Stock Markets and Their Role in Corporate Reform*, Singapore: John Wiley & Sons, 2003

*Jonathan Woetzel, *Capitalist China: Strategies for a Revolutionized Economy*, Singapore: John Wiley & Sons, 2003

Pamela Yatsko, *New Shanghai: The Rocky Rebirth of China's Legendary City,* Singapore: John Wiley & Sons, 2001

David Zweig, *Internationalizing China: Domestic Interests and Global Linkages,* Ithaca: Cornell University Press, 2002

Benjamin Zycher, Nicholas Eberstadt, Charles Wolf Jr, K.C. Yeh, Sung-Ho Lee, *Fault Lines in China's Economic Terrain,* Santa Monica: RAND, 2003

Chinese Literature

Cao Xueqin (Tsao Hsueh Chin), *Dream of the Red Chamber,* New York: Anchor Books, 1989

Pang-Mei Natasha Chang, *Bound Feet and Western Dress,* New York: Anchor Books, 1997

Nien Cheng, *Life and Death in Shanghai,* New York: Penguin Books, 1988

Sue Chun, *Beijing Doll,* London: Abacus, 2004

Bill Holm, *Coming Back Crazy: an Alphabet of China Essays,* Minneapolis: Milkweed Editions, 2000

Jung Chang, *Wild Swans: Three Daughters of China,* New York: Simon & Schuster, 1991

Lin Yutang, *Moment in Peking: a Novel of Contemporary Chinese Life,* New York: J. Day, 1939

*Lin Yutang, *My Country, My People,* New York: Halcyon House, 1939

*Lu Xun, *The Diary of a Madman and Other Stories,* Honolulu: University of Hawaii Press, 1990

Luo Guanzhong and Shi Nai'an, *The Water Margin, or the 108 Heroes,* Singapore: Graham Brash, 1992

*Luo Guanzhong, *Three Kingdoms: a Historical Novel,* Beijing: Foreign Languages Press, 1992

Wei Hui, *Shanghai Baby,* London: Constable & Robinson, 2001

* Favorite personal reads

MAP OF CHINA

Xinjiang

Qinghai

Tibet

Sic

Yun

Huang River

Beijing

Tianjin

Hebei

Shanxi

Ningxia

Shandong

Inner
Mongolia

Heilongjiang

Jilin

Liaoning

Shaanxi

Henan

Jiangsu

Anhui

Shanghai

Chongqing

Yangtze River

Hubei

Zhejiang

Jiangxi

Hunan

Fujian

Guizhou

Xun River

Guangdong

Guangxi

Hong Kong

Macau

Taiwan

Hainan